Horizons

Phonics and Reading

K

Teacher's Guide 3
Lessons 81–120

Author: Pollyann O'Brien, M.A.

Editor: Alan L. Christopherson, M.S.

Alpha Omega Publications, Inc. • Rock Rapids, IA

Printed in the United States of America

ISBN 978-0-7403-0307-4

Scope & Sequence

Lesson 1

Letter **a**
- letter recognition
- short **a** sound
- recognizing and forming uppercase and lowercase **a**

Lesson 2

Letter **b**
- letter recognition
- beginning and ending letter **b** sound
- sound of **ba**
- recognizing and forming uppercase and lowercase **b**

Lesson 3

Letter **d**
- letter recognition
- letter **d** sound
- sound of **dă**
- recognizing and forming uppercase and lowercase **d**

Lesson 4

Letter **o**
- letter recognition
- beginning sound of short **o**
- recognizing and forming uppercase and lowercase **o**
- sound of **lŏ**
- words with short **o** in the middle
- formation of **ba, bo, do, dad**

Lesson 5

Letter **c**
- letter recognition
- sound of letter **c**
- words beginning with **c** and **că**
- recognizing and forming uppercase and lowercase **c**
- formation of **co, ca**

Lesson 6

Letter **e**
- letter recognition
- sound of short **e**
- words with **ĕ** in the middle
- matching phrases to pictures
- beginning sounds **dĕ** and **bĕ**
- word recognition and matching
- recognizing and forming uppercase and lowercase **e**
- matching letter to pictures starting with **ĕ**

Lesson 7

Letter **f**
- letter recognition
- sound of **f**
- beginning sounds **f, fă, fĕ**
- recognizing and forming uppercase and lowercase **f**
- reading and writing "make-up words"
- reading and writing short sentences

Lesson 8

Letter **g**
- letter recognition
- beginning sounds **g, gă, gŏ**
- words beginning and ending in **g**
- auditory discrimination from word list
- recognizing and forming uppercase and lowercase **g**
- matching letter to pictures starting with **g**
- reading and writing "make-up words"
- reading and writing short sentences

Lesson 9

Letter **i**
- letter recognition
- beginning sound of short **i**
- words with short **i** in the middle
- beginning consonant sounds
- middle vowel sounds
- recognizing and forming uppercase and lowercase **i**
- matching letter to pictures starting with **i**

Lesson 10

Letter **h**

- letter recognition
- beginning sounds **h, hă, hĕ, hŏ, hĭ**
- recognizing and forming uppercase and lowercase **h**
- reading and writing "make-up words"
- matching letter to pictures starting with **h**
- adding **s** to make plurals
- capital letter at beginning and period at end of sentence
- matching pictures to phrases

Lesson 11

Letter **u**

- letter recognition
- beginning sounds of **ŭ, dŭ, fŭ, bŭ, cŭ, gŭ**
- words with **ŭ** in the middle
- recognizing and forming uppercase and lowercase **u**
- matching letter to pictures with **ŭ** in the middle
- matching pictures to words

Lesson 12

Letter **t**

- letter recognition
- beginning and ending sound of **t**
- recognizing and forming uppercase and lowercase **t**
- matching letter to pictures starting with **t**
- reading and writing "make-up words"
- reading and printing sentences
- matching pictures to phrases
- recognition and printing **ta, te, ti, to, tu**

Lesson 13

Letter **n**

- letter recognition
- sound of **n, nă**
- matching pictures to words
- recognizing and forming uppercase and lowercase **n**
- matching letters to words starting with **n**
- spelling words to match pictures
- completing sentences with correct word
- printing words and phrases from copy
- identifying pictures starting with **ne, ni, nu, no**
- identifying pictures starting with **an, en, in, un**

Lesson 14

Letter **k**

- letter recognition
- beginning sounds **k, kĭ, kĕ**
- matching pictures to phrases
- recognizing and forming uppercase and lowercase **k**
- printing letters and words with **k**
- reading "make-up words"
- reading and printing sentences

Lesson 15

Letter **l**

- letter recognition
- beginning sounds **l, lă, lĕ, lĭ, lŏ, lŭ**
- ending sound of **l**
- recognizing and forming uppercase and lowercase **l**
- printing letters and words
- completing sentences with correct word
- reading "make-up words"

Lesson 16

Letter **m**

- recognizing and forming uppercase and lowercase **m**
- completing sentences with correct word
- spelling words to match pictures
- reading "make-up words"
- matching pictures to beginning sounds **ma, me, mi, mo, mu**
- reading and printing words and phrases from copy

Lesson 17

Letter **p**

- recognizing and forming uppercase and lowercase **p**
- beginning sounds of **pa, pe, pi, po, pu**
- matching pictures to words
- matching letters to words starting with **p**
- reading "make-up words"
- spelling words to match pictures
- printing words and phrases from copy
- completing sentences with correct word

Lesson 18

Letter **r**

- recognizing and forming uppercase and lowercase **r**
- matching letters to words starting with **r**
- reading "make-up words"
- beginning sounds of **ra, re, ri, ro, ru**
- matching pictures to words
- completing sentences with correct word
- spelling words to match pictures
- printing words and phrases from copy

Lesson 19

Letter **s**

- recognizing and forming uppercase and lowercase **s**
- matching letters to words starting with **s**
- beginning sounds of **sa, se, si, so, su**
- matching pictures to phrases
- recognizing ending sound of **s**
- printing letters, words, and phrases
- completing sentences with correct word

Lesson 20

Letter **q**

- recognizing and forming uppercase and lowercase **q, qu, qui**
- matching letters to words starting with **qu**
- match pictures to words
- reading and writing sentences

Lesson 21

Letter **j**

- recognizing and forming uppercase and lowercase **j**
- matching letters to words starting with **j**
- matching pictures to words
- completing sentences with correct word
- matching pictures to phrases
- beginning sounds of **ja, je, ji, jo, ju**
- spelling words to match pictures
- printing words and phrases from copy

Lesson 22

Letter **v**

- recognizing and forming uppercase and lowercase **v**
- matching letters to words starting with **v**
- spelling words to match pictures
- matching pictures to words and phrases
- beginning sounds of **va, ve, vi, vo, vu**
- completing sentences with correct word
- printing words and phrases from copy
- spelling words to match pictures

Lesson 23

Letter **w**

- recognizing and forming uppercase and lowercase **w**
- matching letters to words starting with **w**
- reading "make-up words"
- matching pictures to words and phrases
- printing words from copy
- completing sentences with correct word
- spelling words to match pictures
- reading and printing sentences

Lesson 24

Letter **y**

- recognizing and forming uppercase and lowercase **y**
- printing letters and words
- matching letters to words starting with **y**
- matching pictures to words and phrases

- completing sentences with correct word
- spelling words to match pictures

Lesson 25

Letter **z**

- recognizing and forming uppercase and lowercase **z**
- matching letters to words starting with **z**
- matching pictures to words
- reading "make-up words"
- recognizing words that end in **z**
- printing letters and words
- completing sentences with correct word
- printing phrases from copy

Lesson 26

Letter **x**

- recognizing and forming uppercase and lowercase **x**
- matching letters to words starting with **x**
- reading "make-up words"
- matching pictures to phrases, sentences, words
- words ending in **x**
- completing sentences with correct word
- spelling words to match pictures
- printing phrases from copy

Lesson 27

Consonant digraph **th**

- rule for beginning consonant digraph **th**
- matching picture to starting sound of **th**
- printing uppercase/lowercase **th**
- reading words/sentences
- identifying puzzle words and phrases
- rhyming and spelling
- reading and printing sentences from copy

Lesson 28

Consonant digraph **th**

- recognize **th** at the beginning or end of a word

- matching pictures to sentences
- printing sentences from copy
- reading "make-up" words
- puzzle words/phrases
- rhyming
- crossword puzzle with missing vowel

Lesson 29

Consonant digraph **ch**

- rule for consonant digraph **ch**
- matching pictures to sound
- using capital letters for names
- printing uppercase/lowercase **ch**
- proper nouns
- reading sentences
- matching words/pictures
- matching puzzle words and phrases
- spelling

Lesson 30

Consonant digraph **wh**

- rule for consonant digraph **wh**
- identify capital and lowercase letters
- identify nonsense words
- create nonsense words from sounds
- printing sentences from copy
- spelling
- use of question mark (?) and words to identify question sentences

Lesson 31

Review **th, ch, wh**

- picture/word review
- picture to sound
- printing
- auditory discrimination from word list
- spelling
- puzzle/"make-up" words and sentences
- recognizing words starting with ch within sentences

Lesson 32

Consonant digraph **sh**
- rule for beginning consonant digraph **sh**
- printing practice with capital and lowercase **sh**
- picture/word match
- puzzle/make-believe words and phrases
- word search
- printing sentences from copy
- rhyming
- spelling

Lesson 33

Consonant digraph **sh**
- rule for **sh** endings
- printing practice with and lowercase **sh**
- picture/beginning sound
- sentences to match picture
- rhyming
- alphabetize
- print sentences from copy
- identify sh at end of word

Lesson 34

Review consonant digraphs **th, ch, wh, sh**
- picture/sound identification
- printing/identifying ending sound
- word/picture identification
- auditory discrimination from word list
- spelling
- printing from copy

Lesson 35

Silent **e: ā e̸**
- rule for silent **e: a e̸**
- picture to sound
- diacritical marking
- short/long **a** contrast
- picture/sentence match
- puzzle/make-believe words and phrases
- spelling
- sentence completion
- word identification without pictures

Lesson 36

Consonant blend **bl**
- rule for blend **bl**
- picture to sound
- printing practice with capital and lowercase **bl**
- printing from copy
- picture to sentence match
- spelling
- word to picture match
- puzzle/make-believe words and phrases
- beginning blend choice

Lesson 37

Consonant blend **br**
- rule for blend **br**
- picture to sound
- printing practice with capital and lowercase **br**
- word identification – diacritical marking
- word/picture identification of sound
- sentence to picture match
- puzzle/make-believe words and sentences
- spelling
- sentence completion
- printing sentence from copy

Lesson 38

Consonant blend **cl**
- rule for blend **cl**
- picture to sound
- printing practice with capital and lowercase **cl**
- word/picture identification for printing
- beginning blend printing/spelling
- picture to word match
- puzzle/make-believe words and phrases
- printing sentence from copy

Lesson 39

Consonant blend **cr**
- rule for consonant blend **cr**
- picture to sound
- printing practice with capital and lowercase **cr**
- picture to word match
- printing beginning sounds
- word/picture identification for printing
- alphabetize
- sentence completion
- puzzle/make-believe words and phrases
- spelling

Lesson 40

Review consonant blends **cr, cl, br, bl**
- word/picture identification
- auditory discrimination from word list
- puzzle/make-believe words and phrases
- spelling – fill in beginning and ending sounds
- sentence printing from copy

Lesson 41

Silent **e:** ī ¢
- rule for silent **e:** ī ¢
- word/picture identification
- diacritical marking
- word/picture match
- sentence/picture match
- puzzle/make-believe words and phrases
- spelling

Lesson 42

Consonant blend **dr** – question sentences
- rule for consonant blend **dr**
- word/picture identification
- practice printing with capital and lowercase **dr**
- word/picture match
- printing beginning sounds for picture
- choice of beginning sounds
- puzzle/make-believe words and phrases

- rule for question marks and sentences
- review of question words and use of question marks
- spelling
- rhyming

Lesson 43

Consonant blend **fl**
- rule for consonant blend **fl**
- practice printing with capital and lowercase **fl**
- beginning sounds identified
- printing beginning sounds
- alphabetical order
- sentence completion
- puzzle/make-believe words and phrases
- sentence printing from copy

Lesson 44

Review silent **e:** ā ¢ and ī ¢ with single consonant beginnings
- review silent e rule
- diacritical marking
- picture/word identification
- printing – place in columns
- word/picture match
- auditory discrimination from word list
- spelling
- sentence completion

Lesson 45

Review silent **e:** ā ¢ and ī ¢ with consonant blend beginnings
- review silent **e** rule
- picture to sound – diacritical markings
- printing – place in columns
- word/picture match
- auditory discrimination from word list
- spelling
- sentence completion from pictures
- sentence completion – original

Lesson 46

Ending **ck**

- rule for **ck** ending
- picture/sound identification
- placement of sound within word
- picture/sentence match
- rhyming
- alphabetical order
- puzzle/make-believe words and phrases
- spelling

Lesson 47

Ending **ing**

- rule for **ing** ending
- picture to sound
- word identification
- picture to word match
- picture/sentence identification and printing
- word completion
- sentence completion
- printing
- auditory discrimination from word list

Lesson 48

Review short and long vowels

- short vowel identification
- long vowel identification
- word/picture match
- puzzle/make-believe words and phrases
- auditory discrimination for word list
- word comprehension from sentence
- spelling

Lesson 49

Silent **e**: ō ¢ – filling in sentences

- rule of silent **e**: ō ¢
- word/picture identification
- printing short and long vowel words - diacritical marking
- word ending choice from pictures
- auditory discrimination from word list

- sentence completion
- rhyming
- puzzle and make believe words
- printing from copy

Lesson 50

Consonant blend **gr**

- rule for consonant blend **gr**
- word/picture match
- practice printing capital and lower case **gr**
- beginning sound identification
- word/picture match
- printing (spelling) beginning sounds from picture
- alphabetical order
- sentence completion
- puzzle/make-believe words and phrases
- word search

Lesson 51

Consonant blend **gl**

- rule for consonant blend **gl**
- word/picture match
- practice printing capital and lower case **gl**
- beginning sound identification
- alphabetical order
- ending sound identification
- auditory discrimination from word list
- sentence completion
- printing sentence from copy

Lesson 52

Consonant blend **sp** – beginning and ending

- rule for consonant blend **sp**
- word/picture match – beginning **sp**
- practice printing **sp** with capital
- word/picture match – ending **sp**
- sentence/picture match
- puzzle/make-believe words and phrases
- spelling and rhyming
- printing sentence from copy

Lesson 53

Consonant digraph ending **tch** and **ch**
- rule for consonant digraph **tch** and **ch**
- word/picture identification of sound
- word/picture match
- discrimination of **ch** and **tch**
- puzzle/make-believe words and phrases
- spelling
- auditory discrimination from word list
- crossword puzzle
- sentence printing from copy

Lesson 54

Review short vowels and silent **e: ā ȩ, ī ȩ, ō ȩ**
- vowel identification
- diacritical marking
- change words from short to long vowel sounds
- words in columns – long **o, i, a**
- word/picture match
- word/sentence match
- rhyming

Lesson 55

Silent **e: ū ȩ**
- review silent **e** rule
- word/picture identification
- print words to match pictures – copy
- sentence completion
- puzzle/make-believe words and phrases
- spelling
- separate columns for long vowel sounds
- auditory discrimination from word list

Lesson 56

Review short and long vowels with blends
- word/picture identification
- beginning or end sound identification
- sentence completion
- rhyming
- printing question sentence from copy

Lesson 57

Review short and long vowels with consonant single and blend beginning
- beginning sound identification/word/picture
- sentence completion
- printing sentence from copy

Lesson 58

Consonant endings **nd**, **nt** – nouns
- rule for consonant endings **nd**, **nt**
- word/picture identification
- printing
- consonant ending discrimination
- auditory discrimination from word list
- rule for nouns – person, thing
- noun identification
- noun recognition of name from sentences
- noun recognition of place from sentences
- word/picture comprehension choice

Lesson 59

Consonant ending **ng** – noun review
- word/picture identification
- printing
- ending sound identification from pictures
- auditory discrimination from word list
- noun identification
- sentence/picture comprehension choice
- rhyming
- printing sentence from copy

Lesson 60

Consonant ending **nk** – writing question sentences
- rule for consonant ending **nk**
- word/picture identification
- printing
- ending discrimination
- auditory discrimination from word list
- sentence completion
- rhyming

- yes/no to question sentences
- printing choice of question sentence

Lesson 61

Review consonant blends **ng**, **nk**, **nd**, **nt**
- word endings identification
- auditory discrimination from word list
- noun identification
- printing
- spelling
- alphabetical order

Lesson 62

Consonant blends **sc** and **sk** beginnings
- rule for consonant blends **sc** and **sk**
- word/picture identification – **sc**
- printing
- word/picture identification – **sk**
- auditory discrimination from word list
- picture/sentence comprehension
- nouns – sentence identification
- sentence comprehension, completion and identification from picture

Lesson 63

Consonant blend **sk** endings
- rule for consonant blend **sk** ending
- work/picture identification
- printing
- word/picture match
- auditory discrimination from word list
- rhyming
- word/picture identification
- spelling
- sentence/picture comprehension
- alphabetical order

Lesson 64

Consonant blend **mp** endings – sentences
- rule for consonant blend **mp** endings
- picture/word identification
- printing
- word/picture discrimination

- auditory discrimination
- rhyming
- rule for description of sentence structure
- exclamation sentences
- question sentences
- statement sentences
- printing choice of sentences from copy

Lesson 65

Consonant ending **lp** – question sentences
- picture/word association
- printing
- picture/word discrimination
- printing choice from pictures – punctuation – question mark – period
- introduction to action words
- writing from copy with choice of action words
- spelling
- auditory discrimination from word list

Lesson 66

Consonant ending **lk** – vocabulary
- rule for consonant ending **lk**
- picture/word discrimination
- spelling choice for sentence completion and comprehension
- auditory discrimination from word list
- word/picture match
- spelling – ending sounds
- picture/sentence comprehension
- printing sentences from copy – punctuation

Lesson 67

Review endings **sk**, **mp**, **lp**, **lk** with short vowels
- picture/ending sound identification
- printing
- spelling
- auditory discrimination from word list
- sentence completion
- alphabetical order

Lesson 68

Review consonant blends

- word/picture identification
- beginning or ending sound discrimination
- spelling
- alphabetical order
- sentence completion
- rhyming
- writing sentence from copy

Lesson 69

Beginning consonant blend **pl** – pronouns

- rule for consonant blend **pl**
- word/picture identification
- practice printing **pl** with capital and lowercase letters
- picture/word beginning sound identification
- picture/word match
- alphabetical order
- Review noun rule
- rule – pronoun
- read sentences – change from noun to pronoun
- write sentence from copy – identify pronoun

Lesson 70

Review beginning consonant blends

- picture/beginning sound identification
- printing
- noun identification
- pronoun identification
- creative sentence making

Lesson 71

Double vowels – **ai**

- rule for double vowels – **ai**
- picture/sound identification
- word/picture match
- print rhyming words from copy
- puzzle/make-believe words and phrases
- sentence completion

- spelling
- printing sentence from copy

Lesson 72

Consonant blends with **ai**

- picture/sound identification
- printing
- puzzle/make-believe words and phrases
- picture/word and sound discrimination
- sentence/picture match
- sentence completion
- alphabetical order

Lesson 73

Consonant blend beginnings **pr**, **tr** – quotation marks

- rule for consonant blend beginnings **pr** and **tr**
- picture/word sound discrimination
- printing
- pictures/choice of beginning sounds
- word/picture match
- rule for quotation marks.
- read sentences
- print sentences using quotation marks

Lesson 74

Consonant blend beginning **sl**

- rule for consonant blend **sl**
- picture/word sound discrimination
- practice printing letters – capital and lowercase
- picture/beginning sound association
- picture/word match
- spelling
- puzzle/make-believe words and phrases
- create puzzle words

Lesson 75

Consonant blend beginning **sm**

- rule for consonant blend **sm**
- picture/word sound discrimination

- practice printing letters – capital and lowercase
- word/picture match
- sentence/picture match
- rhyming
- quotation marks
- spelling
- alphabetical order

Lesson 76

Consonant blend **sn**

- rule for consonant blend **sn**
- picture/word sound discrimination
- practice printing letters – capital and lowercase
- word/picture match
- sentence/picture match
- rhyming
- picture/sentence comprehension
- auditory discrimination from word list

Lesson 77

Review of consonant blends and digraphs

- pictures/sound discrimination
- auditory discrimination from word list
- auditory discrimination identifying ending sounds

Lesson 78

Double vowels – **ea**

- rule for double vowels **ea**
- picture/sound identification
- picture – printing and diacritical marking
- picture/word match
- puzzle/make-believe words and phrases
- rhyming
- sentence completion
- spelling
- printing sentence from copy

Lesson 79

Double vowels – **ee**

- rule for double vowels **ee**
- picture/sound identification

- picture – printing and diacritical marking
- picture/word match
- rhyming
- puzzle/make-believe words and phrases
- sentence/picture match
- spelling
- printing sentence from copy

Lesson 80

Beginning **qu** – picture sequence

- rule for **qu**
- picture/sound identification
- practice printing with capital and lowercase
- picture/word match
- rhyming
- sentence/picture match
- picture sequence

Lesson 81

Beginning blend **scr** – picture sequence

- picture/sound identification
- practice printing with capital and lowercase
- picture/word match
- printing sentence from copy – quotation marks
- spelling
- sentence sequence
- yes/no questions

Lesson 82

Review of double vowels – beginning blends

- picture/sound identification
- auditory discrimination from word list
- spelling
- picture/sentence comprehension
- sentence completion

Lesson 83

Double vowels – **oa**

- review double vowel rule – include **oa**
- picture/sound identification
- printing – diacritical marking

- word/picture match
- rhyming
- puzzle/make-believe words and phrases
- sentence comprehension/pictures
- spelling
- printing sentence from copy

Lesson 84

Beginning blend **fr**
- rule for beginning blend **fr**
- picture/sound identification
- practice printing with capital and lowercase
- picture/word match
- rhyming
- puzzle/make-believe words and phrases
- printing for sentence completion
- spelling
- yes/no sentence
- printing sentence from copy

Lesson 85

Consonant endings **lt**, **lf**
- rule for consonant ending **lt** and **lf**
- picture/sound identification
- reading – sentence comprehension
- auditory discrimination
- spelling
- printing – punctuation
- picture/sentence match

Lesson 86

Consonant ending **ft** – following directions
- rule for consonant ending **ft**
- picture/sound identification
- printing
- word ending sound identification
- auditory discrimination from word list
- picture/sentence comprehension
- follow directions
- word/picture match

Lesson 87

Review consonant endings
- pictures/sound identification
- sentence completion
- rhyme/picture
- auditory discrimination from word list
- spelling

Lesson 88

Review long and short vowel sounds
- picture/sound identification
- change word from short to long – diacritical marking
- column choice for words
- sentence completion

Lesson 89

Consonant blend beginnings **spr**, **spl**
- rule for consonant blend beginnings **spr**, **spl**
- picture/sound identification
- practice printing with capital and lowercase
- picture/sound discrimination
- word to word match
- read sentences from copy – print quotation marks
- alphabetical order
- sentence sequence for story

Lesson 90

Consonant blend beginning **st**
- rule for consonant blend beginning **st**
- picture/sound identification
- practice printing with capital and lowercase
- picture/word match
- rhyming
- puzzle/make-believe words and phrases
- sentence completion
- yes/no choice
- spelling

Lesson 91

Consonant blend review – **tch**, **sp**, **ft**

- ending sound identification
- printing
- picture/sentence comprehension match
- read sentences – vocabulary comprehension
- rhyming
- yes/no choice
- printing sentence from copy

Lesson 92

Consonant blend ending **st**

- rule for consonant blend ending **st**
- printing
- picture/sound identification
- auditory discrimination from word list
- rhyming
- reading sentences – vocabulary enrichment
- spelling
- sentence completion

Lesson 93

Review consonant endings – **tch**, **sp**, **st**, **lt**, **lf**, **ft**

- picture/sound identification
- auditory discrimination from word list
- sentence completion
- rhyming
- spelling – end sounds
- sentence choice to match picture

Lesson 94

Consonant blends **tw**, **sw**

- picture/sound identification
- puzzle/make-believe words and sentences
- printing sentence from copy
- sentence completion
- yes/no choice
- spelling

Lesson 95

Review consonant beginnings **tw**, **sp**, **st**, **spl**, **spr**, **qu**

- picture/sound identification
- auditory discrimination from word list
- sentence completion
- rhyming
- spelling
- yes/no choice
- alphabetical order
- print sentences – quotation marks

Lesson 96

Review endings **lf**, **ft**, **ng**, **nk**, **lk**, **lp**, **sk**, **sh**

- picture/sound discrimination
- sentence completion
- alphabetical order
- spelling
- could be/no way
- columns for endings
- read sentences – vocabulary development

Lesson 97

Vowel plus **r**: **ar**

- rule for vowel plus **r**: **ar**
- picture/sound identification
- practice printing with lowercase
- sentence/picture match – **ar** recognition
- rhyming
- puzzle/make-believe words and phrases
- read sentences – vocabulary development
- word search

Lesson 98

Vowel plus **r**: **or**

- rule for vowel plus **r**: **or**
- picture/sound identification
- practice printing with lowercase
- sentence/picture match – **or** recognition
- puzzle/make-believe words and phrases
- read sentences – vocabulary development
- sentence completion
- printing sentences – capitals/punctuation

Lesson 99

Review vowel plus **r**: **ar, or**

- picture/sound identification
- practice printing
- sentence completion
- alphabetical order
- spelling
- could be/no way
- read sentences – vocabulary development
- auditory discrimination from word list

Lesson 100

Review vowel plus **r**: **ar**

- picture/sound identification
- spelling
- sentence completion
- sentence/picture match – identify **ar**
- puzzle/make-believe words and phrases
- auditory discrimination from word list
- read sentences – vocabulary development

Lesson 101

Review vowel plus **r**: **or**

- picture/sound identification
- spelling
- sentence completion
- alphabetical order
- yes/no choice
- read sentences – vocabulary development
- crossword puzzle

Lesson 102

Vowel plus **r**: **er, ir, ur**

- rule for vowel plus **r**: **er, ir, ur**
- sound identification from written word
- printing
- picture/sentence match – **er** sound identification
- puzzle/make-believe words and phrases
- read sentences – vocabulary development
- could be/no way

Lesson 103

Vowel plus **r**: **ir**

- review rule for vowel plus **r**: **ir**
- sound identification from written word
- printing
- picture/sentence match – **ir** sound identification
- puzzle/make-believe words and phrases
- read sentences – vocabulary development
- auditory discrimination

Lesson 104

Vowel plus **r**: **ur**

- review rule for vowel plus **r**: **ur**
- printing
- picture/sentence match – **ur** sound identification
- puzzle/make-believe words and phrases
- read sentences – vocabulary development
- sound identification

Lesson 105

Review vowel plus **r**: **er, ir, ur**

- picture/sound association
- sentence completion
- printing
- sentence/picture match – sound identification
- words in column
- rhyming
- auditory discrimination from word list
- could be/no way

Lesson 106

Review vowel plus **r**: **ar, or**

- picture/sound association
- sentence completion
- alphabetical order
- picture/sentence match
- words in columns
- yes/no
- rhyming

Lesson 107

Review all vowels plus **r**
- picture/sound association
- sentence completion
- alphabetical order
- rhyming
- picture/sentence match
- word/picture match

Lesson 108

Plurals – **s**
- rule for plurals – **s**
- singular and plural identification
- spelling
- picture/phrase match
- sentence completion
- pictures – choice of plurals or singular

Lesson 109

Plurals – **es**
- rule for plurals – **es**
- spelling
- picture/phrase match
- sentence completion
- pictures – choice of plurals or singular

Lesson 110

Plurals – **y** into **ies**
- rule for **y** into **ies**
- spelling
- picture – plural identification
- phrase/picture match
- sentence completion
- pictures – choice of plurals or singular

Lesson 111

Review plurals – **s**, **es**, **ies**
- plural identification
- spelling
- word identification with plurals
- sentence/picture match – identify plurals

Lesson 112

Review double vowels – **ee**
- review rule for double vowels – **ee**
- picture/sound identification
- print/diacritical markings
- word/picture match
- rhyming
- puzzle/make-believe words and phrases
- sentence comprehension
- spelling
- alphabetical order

Lesson 113

Review double vowels – **ee**, **oa** – apostrophe
- picture/sound association
- printing – diacritical markings
- sentence completion
- spelling
- rhyming
- rule for apostrophe – possession
- sentence exchange – single possession
- sentence exchange – plural possession

Lesson 114

Review double vowels – **ai**, **ea**
- picture/sound association
- column printing
- sentence completion
- spelling
- review apostrophe rule
- sentence exchange – single possession
- sentence exchange – plural possession

Lesson 115

Review all double vowels
- picture/sound association
- printing – diacritical markings
- sentence completion
- puzzle/make-believe words and phrases
- spelling

Lesson 116

Digraph **ay**

- rule for digraph **ay**
- picture/sound association
- printing
- rhyming
- puzzle/make-believe words and phrases
- sentence comprehension
- spelling
- alphabetical order

Lesson 117

Digraph **ey**

- rule for digraph **ey**
- picture/sound association
- printing – diacritical marking
- read sentences – vocabulary development
- rhyming
- puzzle/make-believe words and phrases
- alphabetical order

Lesson 118

Review digraphs **ay**, **ey** – apostrophe

- review digraph rule – **ay**, **ey**
- word/sound association
- sentence completion
- picture/word match
- spelling
- review apostrophe rule
- print sentence exchange for single possession
- print sentence exchange for plural possession

Lesson 119

Diphthong **ow**

- rule for diphthong **ow**
- word/sound association
- picture/word match
- sentence completion
- auditory determination from word list
- printing from copy

Lesson 120

Diphthong **ou**

- rule for both sounds of **ou**
- picture/sound association
- sentence completion
- printing sentences from copy – identify punctuation

Lesson 121

Review digraphs **ay**, **ey**

- picture/sound association
- word/picture match
- spelling
- sentence completion
- noun identification
- sentence sequence
- alphabetical order
- picture/sentence match – **ay**, **ey** identified
- auditory discrimination from word list
- make-believe sentences

Lesson 122

Review digraphs **ay**, **ey**; diphthongs **ow**, **ou**

- picture/word association
- spelling
- sentence completion
- word/picture match – sound identification
- auditory discrimination from word bank
- make-believe phrase

Lesson 123

Digraphs **aw**, **au** – proper nouns – creative writing

- rule for digraphs **aw**, **au**
- picture/sound association
- picture/word match
- word/sound association
- spelling
- sentence completion
- printing – punctuation
- creative writing

- sentence printing – proper nouns
- make-believe phrase

Lesson 124

Digraph **ew**
- rule for digraph **ew**
- picture/sound association
- picture/word match
- spelling
- sentence completion
- review proper nouns
- rule for common noun
- common nouns in sentences
- printing sentences – quotation marks
- auditory discrimination
- make-believe phrase

Lesson 125

Diphthong **oy**
- rule for diphthong **oy**
- picture/sound association
- spelling
- word/picture match
- sentence completion
- proper and common noun identification
- quotation marks
- alphabetical order
- printing
- auditory discrimination from word list

Lesson 126

Review digraphs **aw**, **au**, **ew**; diphthong **oy**
- picture/sound association
- picture/word match
- auditory discrimination from word list
- sentence completion
- printing
- rhyming

Lesson 127

Diphthong **oi**
- rule for diphthong **oi**
- picture/sound association

- picture/word match
- printing
- sentences – sound identification
- make-believe phrases
- spelling
- sentences – vocabulary development
- printing – punctuation

Lesson 128

Review diphthongs **ow**, **ou**; digraphs **ay**, **ey**
- picture/sound association
- sentence completion
- alphabetical order
- rhyming
- sentence/picture match
- printing – punctuation
- auditory discrimination from word list

Lesson 129

Review digraphs **aw**, **au**, **ew**
- picture/sound association
- sentence completion
- picture/word match
- sentences – quotation marks
- auditory discrimination from word list
- spelling
- make-believe phrases

Lesson 130

Review **ow**, **ou**
- picture/sound association
- picture/word match
- spelling
- sentences – sound discrimination
- make-believe phrase
- sentences – punctuation
- auditory discrimination from word list

Lesson 131

Review diphthongs **oy**, **oi**
- picture/sound association
- picture/word match
- spelling

- auditory discrimination from word list
- sentences – sound discrimination
- sentence/picture match
- rhyming
- printing/punctuation

Lesson 132

Letter **y** as in **cry**
- rule for letter **y** as in **cry**
- picture/sound association
- spelling
- word/picture match
- read sentences – vocabulary development
- rhyming
- sentence completion
- auditory discrimination from word list
- printing

Lesson 133

Letter **y** as in **baby**
- rule for Letter **y** as in **baby**
- picture/sound association
- spelling
- word/picture match
- read sentences – vocabulary development
- rhyming
- sentence completion
- auditory discrimination from word list
- printing sentence

Lesson 134

Review Letter **y** as in **cry**, **baby**
- review letter **y** sounds
- picture/sound association
- column printing
- sentence completion
- capitalization – proper nouns
- spelling
- auditory discrimination from word list

Lesson 135

Vowel digraph – special **oo** as in **book**
- rule for vowel digraph – **oo** as in **book**
- picture/printing

- read sentences/sound association
- printing
- auditory discrimination from word list
- rhyming
- read sentences – vocabulary development

Lesson 136

Vowel digraph – special **oo** as in **tooth**
- Rule for vowel digraph – special **oo** as in **tooth**
- picture/printing
- read sentences/sound association
- printing
- auditory discrimination from word list
- rhyming
- read sentences – vocabulary development
- printing sentence from copy

Lesson 137

Review all digraphs/diphthongs
- spelling
- sentence/picture match
- common nouns

Lesson 138

Review letter **y** – long **i** and **e**
- spelling
- sentence completion
- rhyming
- auditory discrimination from word list

Lesson 139

Silent letter **w**
- rule for silent **w**
- picture/word association
- spelling
- printing
- sentences/word identification
- auditory discrimination from word list
- picture description
- make-believe phrase

Lesson 140

Silent letter **k**

- rule for silent **k**
- picture/word association
- spelling
- printing
- make-believe phrase
- auditory discrimination
- sentences – word identification
- picture description

Lesson 141

Silent letter **b**

- rule for silent **b**
- picture/word association
- spelling
- printing
- make-believe phrase
- auditory discrimination from word list
- sentences – word identification
- word discrimination

Lesson 142

Review silent letters **b**, **k**, **w**

- word identification
- word/picture match
- spelling
- auditory discrimination from word list
- sentence/picture match
- identify silent letters
- letter writing

Lesson 143

Silent letter **g**

- rule for silent **g**
- printing
- spelling
- word discrimination
- sentence/picture match
- auditory discrimination from word list
- spelling
- picture description
- questions

Lesson 144

Silent **gh**

- rule for silent **gh**
- word/picture association
- spelling
- phrase match
- auditory discrimination from word list
- sentence/picture match
- puzzle picture

Lesson 145

Review silent letters – **w**, **k**, **b**, **gn**, **gh**

- word/picture identification
- column printing
- auditory discrimination from word list
- word identification
- story comprehension
- creative sentence writing

Lesson 146

le endings

- rule for words ending in le
- word/picture identification
- printing
- word/picture match
- sentence/word identification
- make-believe phrase
- sentence completion
- story comprehension

Lesson 147

Words with **all**

- rule for words with **all**
- word/picture association
- printing
- word/picture match
- spelling
- sentence/word identification
- make-believe phrases
- sentence/comprehension
- story comprehension
- creative sentence writing

Lesson 148

Syllables – double consonants
- rule for double consonants
- word/picture identification
- printing
- sentence/word discrimination

Lesson 149

Syllables – compound words
- rule for syllables with compound words
- word/picture identification
- printing compound words
- word-parts match
- sentences word identification
- make-believe phrase
- word identification
- compound word identification

Lesson 150

Syllables – consonant between vowels
- rule for syllables
- syllable recognition
- printing
- sentences/syllable recognition
- auditory discrimination from word list
- make-believe phrases
- sentences – punctuation
- picture sequence

Lesson 151

Review syllables
- compound word identification
- word/picture match
- sentence completion
- creative sentences using compound words
- creative sentences using double consonants

Lesson 152

Suffix **ing** – prepositions
- signal for word ending with ing
- word/picture match
- spelling
- sentence completion – base word
- rule for prepositions
- picture/identify prepositional phrases

Lesson 153

Special soft **c**
- rule for soft **c**
- reading/printing
- word/picture match
- spelling
- sentences/word identification
- sentence completion
- review noun rule
- identify nouns in sentences
- creative writing of nouns

Lesson 154

Special soft **g**
- rule for soft **g**
- reading/printing
- word/picture match
- spelling
- column printing
- alphabetical order
- make-believe phrases
- sentences/word identification
- picture sequence

Lesson 155

Review ending **ing**, soft **c**, soft **g**
- base word completion
- sentence completion
- picture/word choice
- sentence completion
- sentence sequence
- creative sentence

Lesson 156

Non-phonetic **alk**, **ph** – contractions
- rule for **ph**
- picture/word identification
- printing
- word/picture match

- spelling
- sentence completion
- rule for words with **alk**
- picture/word
- read sentences/vocabulary development
- rule for contractions
- words for contractions
- creative use of contractions

Lesson 157

Non-phonetic **old, ost, olt**

- rule for non-phonetic word parts –
  old, ost, olt
- picture/word identification
- printing
- word/picture match
- read sentences/vocabulary development
- action verbs
- sentence completion
- sentence/picture match – action verb
  identified
- creative action verb

Lesson 158

Non-phonetic **ild, ind**

- rule for non-phonetic word parts – **ild, ind**
- picture/word identification
- printing
- spelling
- sentence completion
- nouns: proper, common
- pronouns
- verbs
- creative sentences

Lesson 159

Review non-phonetic word parts – **alk, old,
ost, olt, ind, ild**

- picture/word match
- printing
- spelling
- picture/word completion choice
- sentence completion
- crossword puzzle
- auditory discrimination

Lesson 160

Review all

- spelling
- plurals
- double vowels
- silent **e**
- picture/word match
- diacritical markings
- double consonants
- syllables
- compound words
- soft **c** and **g**
- picture/word match

Teacher's Lessons

Lesson 81 - Beginning Blend scr

Overview:

- Review beginning sounds
- Introduce beginning blend **scr**
- Review use of quotation marks
- Sentence sequence
- Yes / No questions

Materials and Supplies:

- Teacher's Guide & Student Workbook
- White board
- Reader 3: *The Pet Snake*

Teaching Tips:

Review consonant blends used at the beginning of a word. Use the white board to present the new beginning blend **scr** with both long and short vowels.

Compare the beginnings of **sc** and **scr** to make the student aware of the additional sound. Crisscross ending parts of make-up words so the transition is satisfactory.

Emphasize the blend **scr** sound and have the child imitate as a single sound and as it is used at the beginning of each of the picture words.

Activity 1. Study the pictures and discuss their meaning. Have the student put a circle around each picture that starts with the sound of **scr**.

Pictures: **scrap, brush, screw, scratch
    shrimp, script, scrunch, scram**

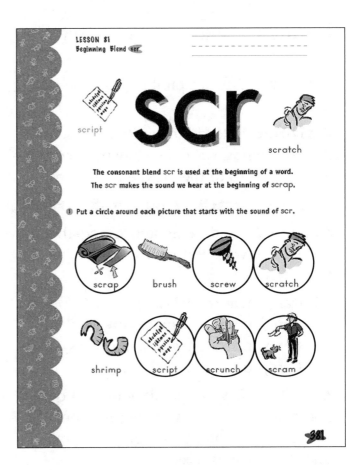

Activity 2. Practice printing **Scr** with a capital **S**.

Activity 3. Practice printing **scr** with a lowercase **s**.

Activities 4. Read the words and discuss their meanings. Have the student draw a line from the word to the picture it matches.

Pictures: **scratch, scrap, scrub, scram**

Activity 5. Read the sentences together. Have the student write **yes** or **no** to the following questions.

1. Can a man scruff? (**no**)
2. Can you scrub a smell? (**no**)
3. Can you scratch your scalp? (**yes**)
4. Can you scrub a van? (**yes**)

Activity 6. Review the placement of quotation marks. Have the student print the following sentences and put the quotation marks that show who is talking.

1. Jack said, ["]I can scrub the van.["]
2. ["]Pick up that scrap,["] said Mom.

Activity 7. Spell the words below the pictures by putting in the beginning sounds.

Pictures: **scr**ipt, **scr**ap, **scr**am

Activity 8. Read the sentences under the pictures with the student. Discuss sequencing: first and last. Have the student put a circle around the sentence that would come LAST in the story.

1. The pup had to scratch at the door.
2. **Mom had to open the door.**

Activity 9. Read the sentences together. Again, discuss sequencing and how the addition of another sentence can change the placement: first, next, and last. Have the student look at the third picture that is added to the story. Which one would come last now? Put a circle around the sentence that would come LAST now.

1. The pup had to scratch at the door.
2. Mom had to open the door.
3. **Mom fed the pup a dish of milk.**

Lesson 82 - Beginning Consonant Blends & Double Vowels

Overview:
- Review beginning consonant blend
- Review double vowels with consonant blend beginnings

Materials and Supplies:
- Teacher's Guide & Student Workbook
- White board
- Reader 3: *Leap in the Sea*

Teaching Tips:
Review all the consonant blends with double and short vowels using the white board as necessary.

Activity 1. Study the pictures together and discuss the beginning sounds of each. Have the student put a circle around the correct beginning consonant blends for each word.

Pictures: **scr**ap, **sk**ip, **sl**ide, **scr**atch
sleep, **sl**ed, **scr**eam, **sk**irt
quack, **sm**ell, **qu**ail, **sn**ail
smash, **qu**een, **sn**iff, **sm**ile

Activity 2. Read one word from each of the boxes and have the student put a circle around the correct word in each box.

Words: **smell, skillet, slip**
snap, scrap, scrub
slap, quit, slept
skid, scream, snip
queen, snail, slide
skit, slip, quit
scrub, sniff, smell
scream, sled, smash

Activity 3. Have the student finish spelling the words by printing the double vowels.

Words: tr**ai**n, gr**ee**n, sp**ea**k
qu**ai**l, h**ea**t, t**ea**m

Activity 4. Have the student spell the words by printing the beginning sounds.

Words: **scr**ub, **sl**ed, **sl**ap
skunk, **qu**een, **sn**iff
slide, **scr**ap, **sm**elt
snail, **sk**ip, **qu**it

Activity 5. Look at the pictures and set of sentences together. Have the student choose the correct sentence to match the picture.

The queen will ride a bike.
The queen will ride on a skunk.

Mr. Smith will slide the team.
Mr. Smith will speak to the team.

Jean can ride on the slide.
Jean can slide on her lap.

The snail is in the scrub.
The snail is on the trail.

Dean's van is green and white.
Dean's van is bean and whip.

Jake likes to skip on the sniff.
Jake likes to skip near the train.

④ Spell the words by printing the beginning sounds.

scr ub   sl ed   sl ap

sk unk   qu een   sn iff

sl ide   scr ap   sm elt

sn ail   sk ip   qu it

387

⑤ Look at the set of sentences below. Underline the correct sentence to match the picture.

The queen will ride a bike.
The queen will ride on a skunk.

Mr. Smith will slide the team.
Mr. Smith will speak to the team.

Jean can ride on the slide.
Jean can slide on her lap.

The snail is in the scrub.
The snail is on the trail.

Dean's van is green and white.
Dean's van is bean and whip.

Jake likes to skip on the sniff.
Jake likes to skip near the train.

388

Activity 6. Read the sentences and words together. Have the student finish the sentences by printing words from the word bank.

1. I like to ride on a (**train**).
2. The skunk can (**smell**) bad.
3. Dean can hop as fast as a (**snail**) can run.
4. Jean said, "The (**quail**) can fly."
5. Did you hear the man (**scream**)?
6. The queen sat on a (**chair**).
7. Dave can jump in a (**deep**) lake.

Activity 7. Read the sentences together. Again, discuss sequencing and how the addition of another sentence can change the placement: first, next, and last. Have the student look at the third picture that is added to the story. Which one would come last now? Put a circle around the sentence that would come LAST now.

1. Dad said, "Mom, that was a good meal. I like to eat."
2. **Mom said, "I see scraps of meat on a plate."**

Activity 8. Read the sentences together. Again, discuss the sequence of sentences and how the addition of a sentence can change the placement: first, next, or last. Have the student read the sentences alone and put a circle around the sentence that would come LAST in the story now.

1. Dad said, "Mom, that was a good meal. I like to eat."
2. Mom said, "I see scraps of meat on a plate."
3. **Mom said, "I will scrub the dishes and then sit on the bench."**

Lesson 83 - Double Vowels oa

Overview:

- Review double vowels **ai**, **ea**, and **ee**
- Introduce double vowel **oa**

Materials and Supplies:

- Teacher's Guide & Student Workbook
- White board
- Reader 3: *Billy, the Goat*

Teaching Tips:

Review the Double Vowel Rule: When two vowels are close together, the first one is long (says its own name) and the second one is silent. Use the white board to demonstrate the double vowels **oa** with single consonants and beginning blends.

Activity 1. Study the pictures and discuss their meanings. Have the student put a circle around those that have the long **o** sound.

> Pictures: **toast, boat, train, soap
> beet, toad, roast, road**

Activity 2. Read the words and identify the pictures together. On the lines below, have the student print the words that match the picture. Cross out the second vowel and make a straight line over the first vowel to show that it has a long sound.

> Pictures: **coat, soak, boat
> groan, loaf, soap
> roast, road, goat**

Activity 3. Study the pictures and read the words together. Have the student draw a line from the word to match the picture:

    Pictures: **roast, boat, coat, soak, loaf, toad**

Activity 4. Have the student print the words that rhyme.

    goat/**coat, boat, float**
    toad/**road**
    toast/**roast, boast, coast**

Activity 5. Have the student read the make-up words.

    Make-up Words: **boak, toap, fload, joam**

Activity 6. Read the puzzle phrases together. Have the student draw a line from the puzzle picture to the phrase it matches.

    Pictures: **a roach on the coach**
               a goat with toast
               a coat on a boat
               roast the toad

Activity 7. Read the sentences together and discuss the pictures. Have the student draw a line under the sentence that matches the picture.

Bill went with us for a ride in a boat.
Bill went with us for a ride on the toast.

Mom can fix a toad for the soap.
Mom can fix a roast for the lunch.

Dave will coach the team.
Dave will roach the team.

Mr. Sloan had a loaf for us.
Mr. Sloan had a groan for us.

Activity 8. Have the student practice printing the sentence on the white board. Then the student will print the sentence in the student workbook.

    Sentence: **My goal is to read well.**

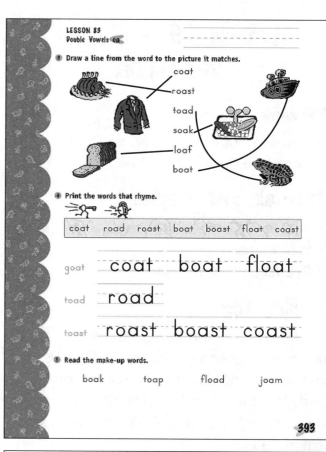

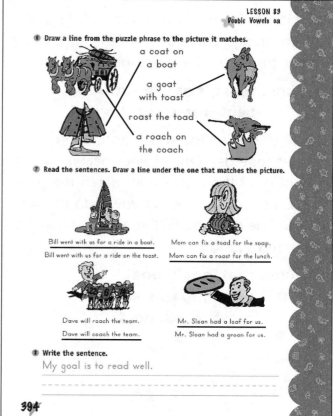

Lesson 84 - Beginning Consonant Blend fr

Overview:
- Review beginning consonant blends
- Introduce beginning consonant blend **fr**
- Spelling
- Yes / No sentences

Materials and Supplies:
- Teacher's Guide & Student Workbook
- White board
- Reader 3: *Loaf, the Watch Dog*

Teaching Tips:
Review consonant blends used at the beginning of a word. Use the white board to present the new beginning blend **fr** with short vowels.

Activity 1. Study the pictures and together discuss the meanings. Have the student put a circle around each picture that starts with the sound of **fr**.

Pictures: **frog, front, fox, fruit freeze, print, fry, frizz**

Activity 2. Practice printing **Fr** with a capital **F**.

Activity 3. Practice printing **fr** with a lower-case **f**.

Activity 4. Read the words and discuss their meaning. Have the student draw a line from the word to the picture it matches.

Pictures: **frog, froth, frost, frizz**

Activity 5. Read the make-up words.

Make-up Words: **frob, fras, fren, frup, frod**

Activity 6. Read the rhyming words together. Have the student print the words that rhyme.

frog/**log, cog, dog**
free/**bee, see, Dee**
fry/**my, shy, cry**
Fred/**Ted, bed, red**

Activity 7. Read the puzzle phrases together. Have the student draw a line from the phrase to the picture it matches.

Pictures: **frost on a dog**
Fred with a frizz
froth on a moth
a sock on a frog

Activity 8. Read the sentences and the words from the word bank together. Have the student print the word in the blank to complete the sentence.

1. The **frog** was in the pond.
2. The **frost** was on the grass.
3. Fed and Ted ate **fresh** fruit.
4. Jill had a **frill** on her dress.

Activity 9. Read the sentences. Put a circle around the **yes** if the sentence is true. Circle **no** if the sentence is not true.

1. Is a frog as big as a log? (**no**)
2. Is the frost hot? (**no**)
3. Can you drink broth?(**yes**)
4. Can you get a note from mom? (**yes**)

Activity 10. Spell the words under the pictures by filling in the beginning sounds.

Pictures: **fr**og, **br**oke, **gr**ass
cloth, **cl**amp, **sl**ip

Activity 11. Have the student practice printing the sentence. Then the student is to print it in his student workbook.

Sentence: **I am glad I can sit in front.**

Activity 12. Have the student spell the words under the pictures by filling in the beginning and the end sounds.

Pictures: **t**oa**d**, **c**oa**t**, **r**oa**d**
boa**t**, **s**oa**p**, **g**oa**t**

Lesson 85 - Ending Consonant Blends: lt, lf

Overview:

- Review capital letters for beginning a sentence and person's name
- Introduce ending consonant blend **lt, lf**
- Spelling
- Punctuation with periods and question marks

Materials and Supplies:

- Teacher's Guide & Student Workbook
- White board
- Reader 3: *The Little Elf*

Teaching Tips:

Using the white board, demonstrate the change from **ll** ending (**bell**) to a **lt** ending (**belt**); (**shell**) change to (**shelf**). Review capitalization as used at the beginning of a sentence and proper nouns. Review periods and question marks.

Activity 1. Study the pictures and discuss the meanings for vocabulary development. Have the student put a CIRCLE around the pictures that have the sound of **lt** at the end of the word. Put a SQUARE around the pictures that have the sound of **lf**.

Pictures: **belt, tilt, bell, shelf
self, malt, salt, wilt**

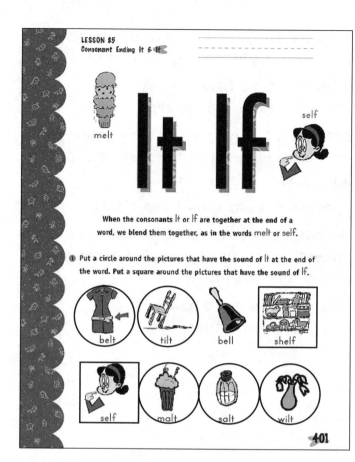

Horizons Kindergarten Phonics

Activity 2. Read the sentences together and discuss vocabulary meanings and spelling of words from Activity 1.

1. Spell the word if you want something to put around your waist. (**belt**)

2. Spell the word if it goes with pepper to season your food. (**salt**)

3. Spell the word if you want to put something on a special place. (**shelf**)

4. Spell the word if a flower does not get enough water. (**wilt**)

5. Spell the word if you want something sweet with milk to drink. (**malt**)

6. Spell the word if you want something that is on a slant. (**tilt**)

Activity 3. Read one word from each of the boxes and have the student put a circle around the correct word in each box.

Words: **milk, elk, salt**
       shelf, ramp, self
       melt, silk, hulk
       lamp, camp, wilt

Activity 4. Discuss the pictures and possible endings for the spelling words.

Pictures: mi**lk**, e**lk**, sa**lt**
        she**lf**, ra**mp**, se**lf**
        me**lt**, si**lk**, hu**lk**
        la**mp**, ca**mp**, wi**lt**

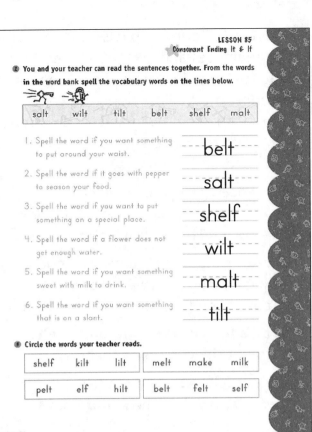

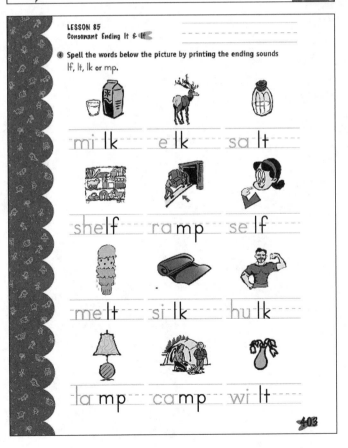

Activity 5. Review capitalization for beginning sentences and person's names. Read the sentences together. Have the student print the sentences on the lines using the correct capital letters at the beginning and for a person's name. Use the correct period or question mark at the end of the sentence.

    Sentences: **D**id you see an elf**?**
                  Jane has a belt on her dress**.**
                  The plant will wilt**.**

Activity 6. Read the sentences together and study the pictures. Have the student underline the correct sentence to match the picture.

Fred's ice cream cone will melt.
Sam put the lamp on a shelf.

The tot felt sad when she fell.
Ted put on elf pants and socks.

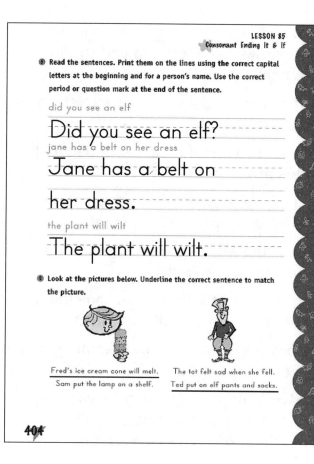

Lesson 86 - Ending Consonant Blend: ft

Overview:

- Review beginning and ending blends
- Auditory direction following: left/right discrimination - shape knowledge
- Introduce ending blend **ft**

Materials and Supplies:

- Teacher's Guide & Student Workbook
- White board
- Reader 3: *Who Got the Gift?*

Teaching Tips:

Introduce ending consonant blend **ft**. Using the white board, combine various beginnings to make words ending with **ft**.

The following auditory directions will help establish left/right handedness.

Activity 1. Study the pictures and words. Discuss the meanings for vocabulary development. Have the student put a circle around the pictures that have the sound of **ft** at the end of the word.

Pictures: **flag, raft, left, gift soft, lift, rest, sift**

Activity 2. Print the words you have circled in Activity 1.

Words: **raft, left, gift, soft, lift, sift**

Activity 3. Study the pictures and determine the sound ending for each picture. Circle the correct ending for each of the pictures below.

Pictures: gi**ft**, te**nt**, me**lt** she**lf**, ha**nd**, se**nd**

Activity 4. Read one word from each of the boxes and have the student put a circle around the correct word in each box.

Words: **raft, tent, fond, mend, elf, malt felt, wilt, soft, sand, tent, shelf**

Activity 5. Read the sentences together and study the picture. Have the student underline the sentence that matches the picture.

The raft was on the pond.
The raft was in the pan.

This is my sand hand.
This is my left hand.

The dress is made of soft cloth.
The lint is made of soft cloth.

Mom had to lift to make the cake.
Mom had to sift to make the cake.

Activity 6. Establish the left/right handedness in the student as well as knowledge of shapes and sizes. Read the following directions to him and observe the response.

1. **Put your left pointer finger on the big square.**
2. **Put your left pointer finger on a small circle.**
3. **Print your name in the large triangle.**
4. **Put your right hand over the small square.**
5. **Put your right thumb on the large square.**
6. **Put your left hand under the small triangle.**
7. **Put your right hand on top of the small triangle.**
8. **Put your left thumb at the top of the large triangle.**
9. **At the bottom of the exercise print: "I like to go to school."**

Activity 7. Have the student compare the words in each column, then draw a line from the words in the left column to the matching words in the right column.

Words: **raft, frog, ant, runt, shelf, belt**

42

Lesson 87 - Review Consonant Blend Endings

Overview:

- Review ending consonant blends
- Pictures and words that rhyme
- Spelling

Materials and Supplies:

- Teacher's Guide & Student Workbook
- White board
- Reader 3: *Hank's New Clothes*

Teaching Tips:

For review, have the student print the ending sounds he hears at the end of the words dictated.

Activity 1. Circle the letters that make the ending sound you hear.

Pictures: ha**nd**, chi**ck**, sa**nd**
churr**ch**, si**ck**, ri**ng**

Activity 2. Circle the letters that make the ending sound you hear.

Pictures: ca**tch**, a**nt**, ba**ng**
mi**lk**, si**nk**, ha**ng**

Activity 3. Circle the letters that make the ending sound you hear.

Pictures: la**mp**, she**lf**, wi**lt**
de**sk**, se**lf**, ca**mp**

Activity 4. Circle the letters that make the ending sound you hear.

Pictures: le**ft**, wa**sp**, too**th**
ba**th**, ra**ft**, di**sh**

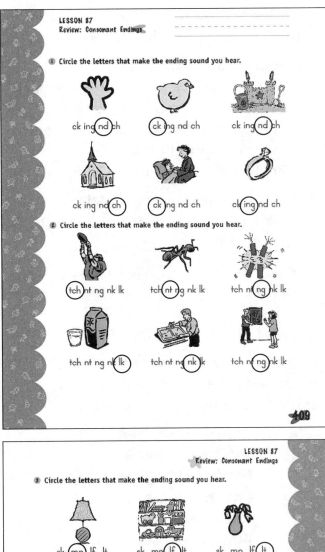

Activity 5. Read the sentences. Choose the correct word to fill in the blanks.

1. Tom used his (**left**) hand to print.
2. The tot was sick and had the (**mumps**).
3. Mom can fix the (**clasp**) for Jan.
4. The hen had ten (**chicks**) in her nest.
5. Jack can (**spin**) his rope.
6. Brent had a (**tent**) at the camp.

Activity 6. Read the words under the pictures. Have the student draw a line from the pictures that rhyme.

game/**flame**	shake/**rake**
yell/**bell**	hear/**ear**
mail/**sail**	smell/**tell**
quick/**trick**	trip/**drip**

Activity 7. Read one word from each of the boxes and have the student put a circle around the correct word in each box.

Words: **lamp, mask, belt**
soft, milk, bunk
bank, runt, gang
ant, hung, pond
tank, raft, silk
limp, melt, self

Horizons Kindergarten Phonics

Lesson 88 - Review Long and Short Vowels

Overview:

- Review short vowels, silent **e** words and double vowels
- Review change from short vowels to silent **e**
- Put words in columns

Materials and Supplies:

- Teacher's Guide & Student Workbook
- White board
- Reader 3: *The Toad*

Teaching Tips:

For review, have the student use the white board while taking dictation of words using short vowels and changing words with silent **e**.

Explain putting words in columns: all short vowels; all silent **e** columns.

Activity 1. Study the pictures and identify the words under them. Have the student put a CIRCLE around the pictures that have the sound of long **a**. Put a SQUARE around the pictures that have the sound of long **e**.

Long **a**: **maid, train, jail**

Long **e**: **peach, hear, bead, beach, speak**

Activity 2. Study the pictures and identify the words under them. Have the student put a CIRCLE around the pictures that have the sound of long **a**. Put a SQUARE around the pictures that have the sound of short **a**.

Long **a**: **pail, paint, rain, chain**

Short **a**: **rack, pal, cat, Sam**

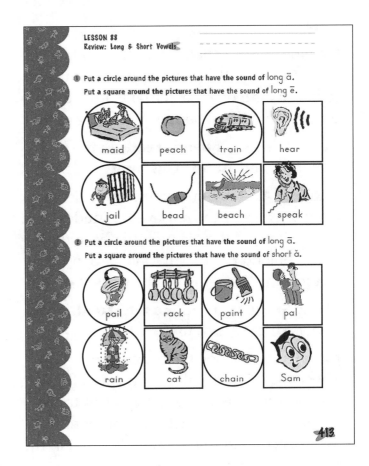

Activity 3. Study the pictures and identify the words under them. Have the student put a CIRCLE around the pictures that have the sound of long **e**. Put a SQUARE around the pictures that have the sound of short **e**.

Long **e**: **leak, queen, read, leaf**
Short **e**: **red, send, Ted, met**

Activity 4. Study the pictures and identify the words under them. Have the student put a CIRCLE around the pictures that have the sound of long **o**. Put a SQUARE around the pictures that have the short sound of **o**.

Long **o**: **goat, road, coach, toad, coat**
Short **o**: **cot, rod, lock**

Activity 5. Change the word from a short vowel into a word with a long vowel by adding a silent **e**. Student may want to use the white board to practice. Then print the words according to the example given in the instructions to the student.

Words:	hid	**hidé**	**hide**
	pal	**palé**	**pale**
	cut	**cuté**	**cute**
	plan	**plané**	**plane**
	rat	**raté**	**rate**
	pin	**piné**	**pine**
	rid	**ridé**	**ride**

Activity 6. Illustrate printing words in a short vowel column, and in a second column, print words with silent **e**.

Have the student print the words from the word bank in the correct columns.

Short Vowel Words:
> **rip, hop, rod, mad, rat, cut, cod, pet, rob**

Long Vowel Words:
> **Pete, cute, rate, rode, ripe, code, robe, made, hope**

Activity 7. Print the correct word in the blanks in the sentences.

1. The sun (**shone**) on the lake.
2. Dad can fix eggs in the camp (**tent**).
3. Mom said, "Do not (**smoke**)."
4. June is a (**cute**) girl.
5. The kids rode on the (**tube**) in the lake.
6. Jane ate a big (**cake**).
7. Jan put the bud in a (**vase**).
8. I can (**dive**) in the lake.
9. The little kids fuss and (**whine**).

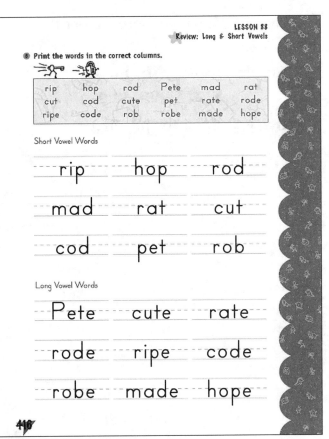

Activity 8. Spell the words under the pictures.

Pictures: **milk, dish, hand
ant, camp, dog**

Activity 9. Color the picture.

Lesson 89 - Beginning Consonant Blends: spr, spl

Overview:

- Introduce beginning consonant blends: **spr**, **spl**
- Review alphabetical order
- Four story/picture sequence
- Review quotation marks

Materials and Supplies:

- Teacher's Guide & Student Workbook
- White board
- Reader 3: *Hidden Word Puzzle Story*

Teaching Tips:

Review consonant blends used at the beginning of a word. Use the white board to present the new beginning consonant blends **spr** and **spl**. Compare the beginnings of words with **sp** beginning as **sp**out, then begin the same ending with **spr** – **spread**, **spl** – **splice**, **splint**.

Activity 1. The consonant blend **spr** is used at the beginning of the word. The **spr** makes the sound we hear at the beginning of the word **sprinkle**. Study the pictures and words together. Put a circle around each picture that starts with the sound **spr**.

Pictures: **spring, sprout, spray, Spot spruce, spread, speak, sprinkle**

Activity 2. Practice printing **Spr** with a capital **S** and **spr** with a lower case **s**.

Activity 3. The consonant blend **spl** is used at the beginning of a word. The **spl** makes the sound we hear at the beginning of **splash**. Put a circle around each picture that starts with the sound of **spl**.

Pictures: **splash, splint, slam, split speak, skip, splinter, splice**

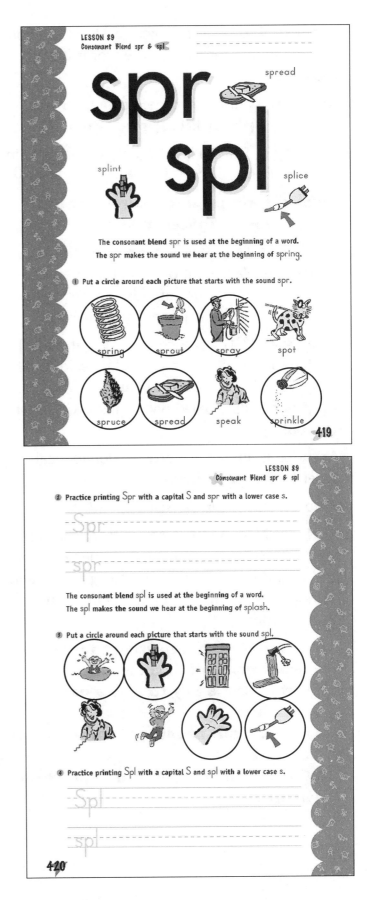

Activity 4. Practice printing **Spl** with a capital **S** and **spl** with a lower case **s**.

Activity 5. Look at the pictures. Print the correct beginning for each of the words below the pictures.

Pictures: **spl**ash, **spr**inkle, **spr**out, **spr**ing **spl**it, **spl**ice, **spr**ead, **spl**inter

Activity 6. Draw a line to match the words in each column.

Words: **spring, sprout, spruce, split, splint, splice, splinter**

Activity 7. Read the sentences together. Review the placement of quotation marks. Have the student put quotation marks around the words that show people are speaking.

Dad said, ["]The spruce tree will get big.["]
["]I had a splinter in my hand,["] said Brad.
Jack said, ["]I can splash you!["]
["]Get back!["] yelled Bill. ["]Jack will splash you!["]

Activity 8. Print the words in alphabetical order in the spaces below.

Words: **pink, quick, spring, think**

Activity 9. Study the pictures that make up the story. Write 1 under the first one; 2 under the second one; 3 under the third picture; and 4 under the last one to tell the story in the correct order.

1. **Girl getting a step stool to reach a board game off a shelf.**
2. **Girl asking a boy to play a game with her.**
3. **Boy and girl opening the box to play a game.**
4. **Game is finished. Boy and girl shake hands.**

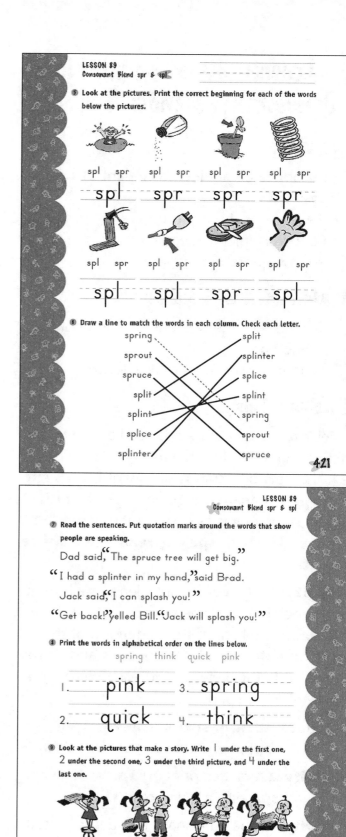

Lesson 90 - Beginning Consonant Blend: st

Overview:

- Review rhyming words
- Yes / No sentences
- Spelling
- Introduce beginning consonant **st**

Materials and Supplies:

- Teacher's Guide & Student Workbook
- White board
- Reader 3: *Stan's Stack of Stuff*

Teaching Tips:

Review consonant blends used at the beginning of a word. Use the white board to present the new beginning consonant blend **st**.

Activity 1. The consonant blend **st** is used at the beginning of a word. The **st** makes the sound we hear at the beginning of **stamp**. Study the pictures and words together. Put a circle around each picture that starts with the sound **st**.

Pictures: **stairs, split, stamp, stick slide, stump, stitch, stag**

Activity 2. Practice printing **St** with a capital **S** and **st** with a lower case **s**.

Activity 3. Read the words together and discuss the meaning of the pictures for vocabulary development. Have the student draw a line from the word to the picture it matches.

Pictures: **stag, stunk, step, stand, sting**

Activity 4. Read the make-up words.

Make-up Words: **staj, slod, spug, sprib, splen**

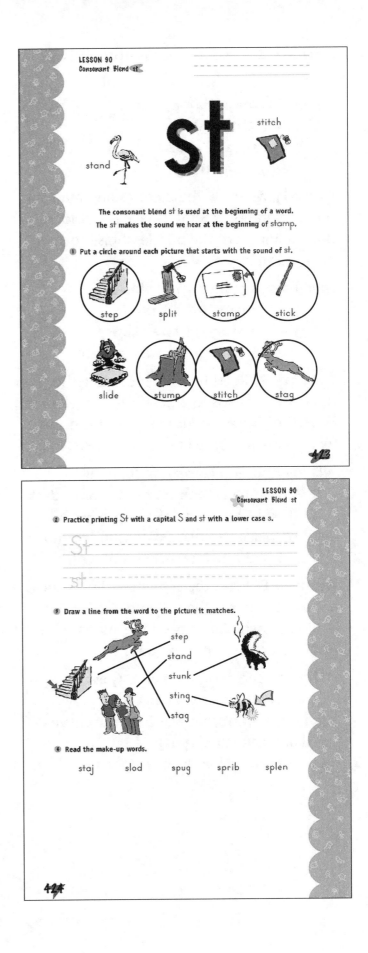

Activity 5. Print the words from the word bank that rhyme.

stamp/**tramp, ramp, camp**
stilt/**kilt, tilt, wilt**
stab/**crab, cab, grab**
stag/**tag, rag, drag**

Activity 6. Study the pictures and read the puzzle phrases together. Have the student draw a line from the puzzle phrase to the picture it matches.

Pictures: **a stunt on a planet**
a dog on stilts
a stag on the steps
a stamp on Sam's nose

Activity 7. Read the sentences together and discuss the words for vocabulary development. Have the student print the word from the word bank to complete the sentence.

1. Jean put a (**stamp**) on the mail.
2. Dad had a (**stack**) of notes on his desk.
3. The dog had a (**stick**) to play with.
4. The black van was (**stuck**) in the mud.
5. Dan had much (**stuff**) on his cot.

Activity 8. Read the sentences. Put a circle around the **yes** if the statement is true or could happen. Circle **no** if the statement is not true or could not happen.

The bee can sting my hand. (**yes**)
I can slide on a stem. (**no**)
Jim did a stunt that was fun to see. (**yes**)
A skunk can stink. (**yes**)
I stand on my hands to sleep. (**no**)

Lesson 91 - Review Ending Blends: sp, ft, tch

Overview:
- Review of ending blends: **sp**, **ft**, **tch**
- Yes / No sentences

Materials and Supplies:
- Teacher's Guide & Student Workbook
- White board
- Reader 3: *The Camp Cook*

Teaching Tips:
Review all the pictures with the student before beginning each activity. Emphasis should be made on the ending sounds. Use the white board to assist in review any of the words in question.

Activity I. Study the pictures together and discuss the meaning of each for vocabulary development and review. Have the student circle the letters that make the sound you hear at the end of each word.

Pictures: ca**tch**, cla**sp**, ma**tch**, ra**ft**
gi**ft**, ha**tch**, la**tch**, gra**sp**

Activity 2. Print the letters that make the ending sounds you hear.

Pictures: she**lf**, gi**ft**, wi**lt**
e**lk**, me**lt**, si**ft**
sa**ng**, ba**nk**, ca**mp**
ba**ng**, bu**nk**, ra**mp**

Activity 3. Read the sentences together and discuss the meaning of each. Have the student underline the sentence that matches the picture.

The glass is in a spill.
The ranch is on a hill.

Mom gave a gift to Dad.
Dad gave a sift to Mom.

The bank took Sam to the dimes.
Sam took the dimes to the bank.

Don can grasp the rope.
Don will shelf the rope.

Activity 4. Print the words that rhyme.

catch/**match, hatch**
bent/**dent, sent**
gift/**lift, shift**

Activity 5. Read the sentences together and discuss the words in the word box.

1. The boy will (**catch**) the ball.
2. The (**wasp**) can sting me.
3. I (**left**) my bat at the game.
4. Sam had a (**gift**) for his mom.
5. Can you (**match**) the red and black cloth?
6. Meg can (**grasp**) the cup.

Activity 6. Write the sentence.

Sentence: **I am glad God loves me.**

Read the sentences. Underline the sentence that matches the picture.

The glass is in a spill.
The ranch is on a hill.

Mom gave a gift to Dad.
Dad gave a sift to Mom.

The bank took Sam to the dimes.
Sam took the dimes to the bank.

Don can grasp the rope.
Don will shelf the rope.

Print the words that rhyme.

| match | lift | dent | sent | hatch | sift |

catch   **match**   **hatch**

bent   **dent**   **sent**

gift   **lift**   **sift**

429

You and your teacher can read the sentences together. From the words in the word bank, spell the vocabulary words on the lines below.

| wasp | catch | match | gift | left | grasp |

1. The boy will **catch** the ball.

2. The **wasp** can sting me.

3. I **left** my bat at the game.

4. Sam had a **gift** for his mom.

5. Can you **match** the red and black cloth?

6. Meg can **grasp** the cup.

Write the sentence.
I am glad God loves me.

430

Lesson 92 - Ending Consonant Blend: st

Overview:

- Introduce ending consonant blend **st**
- Word meanings from sentence description

Material and Supplies:

- Teacher's Guide & Student Workbook
- White board
- Reader 3: *The Best Pest*

Teaching Tips:

Use the white board in introducing the ending blend **st** with other beginning parts of words. Present the sound **st** makes at the end of the word, as in **fast** and **west**.

Activity 1. Study the pictures and words. Discuss the meaning of each for vocabulary development. Have the student put a circle around the pictures that have the sound of **st** at the end of the word.

> Pictures: **rest, dust, fast, cast, west, boat, vest, nest**

Activity 2. Print any five of the six words from the word bank.

> Words: **west, vest, nest, pest, cast, dust**

Activity 3. Study the pictures and the ending sounds of each. Have the student put a circle around the correct ending for each of the pictures below.

> Pictures: ca**st**, she**lf**, le**ft**
> du**st**, be**lt**, fi**st**

Activity 4. Read one word from each of the boxes and have the student put a circle around the correct word in each box.

> Words: **fast, elf, tilt**
> **golf, west, disk**
> **wilt, test, sift**
> **lost, salt, melt**

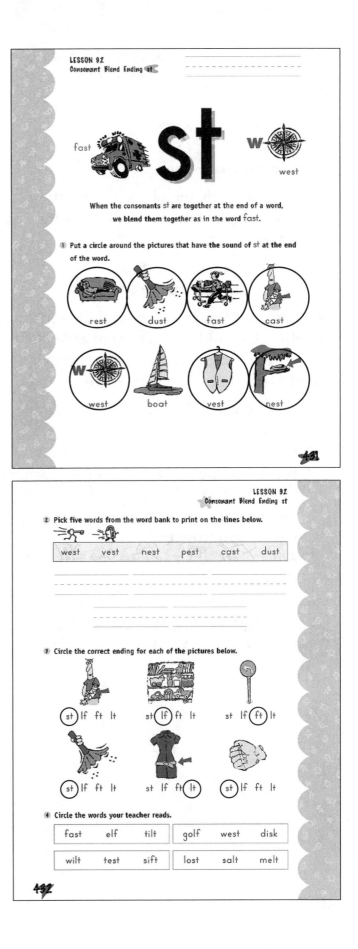

Activity 5. Read the words in the word bank. Write the words that rhyme on the lines below.

nest/**pest, test, rest**
fast/**mast, cast, last**
just/**dust, rust, must**

Activity 6. Study the pictures. Spell the words below the pictures by filling in the first two letters.

Words: **fi**st, **ca**st, **ne**st, **fa**st,
　　　rest, **ve**st, **ru**st, **co**st

Activity 7. Read the words and the sentences together. Discuss the meaning of each. Print the word in the blank that means the same thing as described in the sentence.

1. A place where baby birds hatch is a (**nest**).
2. Doctors fix broken arms with a (**cast**).
3. A piece of metal that is left in the rain and air will (**rust**).
4. When you really have to do something, we say you (**must**) do it.
5. A better job than anyone else is the (**best**).
6. A jacket without sleeves is a (**vest**).
7. The direction in which the sun sets in the evening is the (**west**).

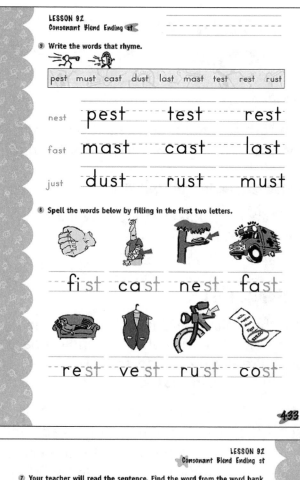

Horizons Kindergarten Phonics

Activity 8. Look at the words in the word bank. Print the word on the lines that makes the sentence correct.

1. Jon was mad. He made a (**fist**) with his hand.
2. Ted broke his leg and Dr. Moss fixed it with a (**cast**).
3. The nail was left out in the rain. We could see the (**rust**) on it.

Activity 9. Read the sentences. Put a circle around the **yes** if the statement is true or could happen. Circle **no** if the statement is not true or could not happen.

Ben felt a lump in his cot. (**yes**)
A little red bug is a good gift. (**no**)
Bill had to limp when he had his stilts. (**no**)
The cone can melt in the sun. (**yes**)
Brent put the belt on his pants. (**yes**)

Activity 10. Spell the words under the pictures by filling in the beginning sounds.

Pictures: **st**amp, **sl**ip, **ch**ick
       stag, **st**ump, **qu**een
       stack, **spl**ash, **fr**og

Lesson 93 - Review Ending Consonant Blends: tch, sp, st, lt, ft

Overview:

- Review ending consonant blends – **tch, sp, st, lt, ft**
- Review rhyming
- Review sentence
- Choice from pictures

Materials and Supplies:

- Teacher's Guide & Student Workbook
- White board
- Reader 3: *The Chest for Fish*

Teaching Tips:

In each activity, review the pictures and ending sounds.

Activity 1. Study the pictures and discuss the ending sounds. Have the student put a circle around the pictures that have the ending sound of **tch**.

Pictures: **catch, smash, hatch, pitch patch, shave, ditch, match**

Activity 2. Study the pictures and discuss the ending sounds. Have the student put a circle around the pictures that have the ending sound of **sp**.

Pictures: **clasp, spell, fast, crisp, hasp, gasp, wasp, swim**

Activity 3. Study the pictures and discuss the ending sounds. Have the student put a circle around the pictures that have the ending sound of **st**.

Pictures: **rest, test, nest, hunt**
melt, dust, vest, scrap

Activity 4. Study the pictures and discuss the ending sounds. Have the student put a circle around the pictures that have the ending sound of **lt**.

Pictures: **belt, wilt, bell, salt**
frog, malt, melt, stamp

Activity 5. Read one word from each of the boxes and have the student put a circle around the correct word in each box.

Words: **match, slip, fist**
list, fast, mist
milk, lisp, spring
quill, lift, mast

Activity 6. Study the words and discuss the ending sounds. Have the student put a circle around the pictures that have the ending sound of **ft**.

Pictures: **raft, gift, slip, flag**
dump, melt, sift, left

Activity 7. Spell the words under the pictures by printing the ending sounds.

Words: ca**tch**, ma**st**, wi**lt**, she**lf**
ha**tch**, fa**st**, me**lt**, e**lk**

Activity 8. Print the words from the word bank that rhyme with the words listed below.

bunch/**munch, lunch**
fast/**cast, mast**
catch/**patch, hatch**
mask/**ask, task**

Activity 9. Read the sentences. Choose the correct word to fill in the blanks.

1. Jack can run (**fast**).
2. Don lives on a (**ranch**).
3. The little chicks will (**hatch**) in a week.
4. Mom made the toast (**crisp**).

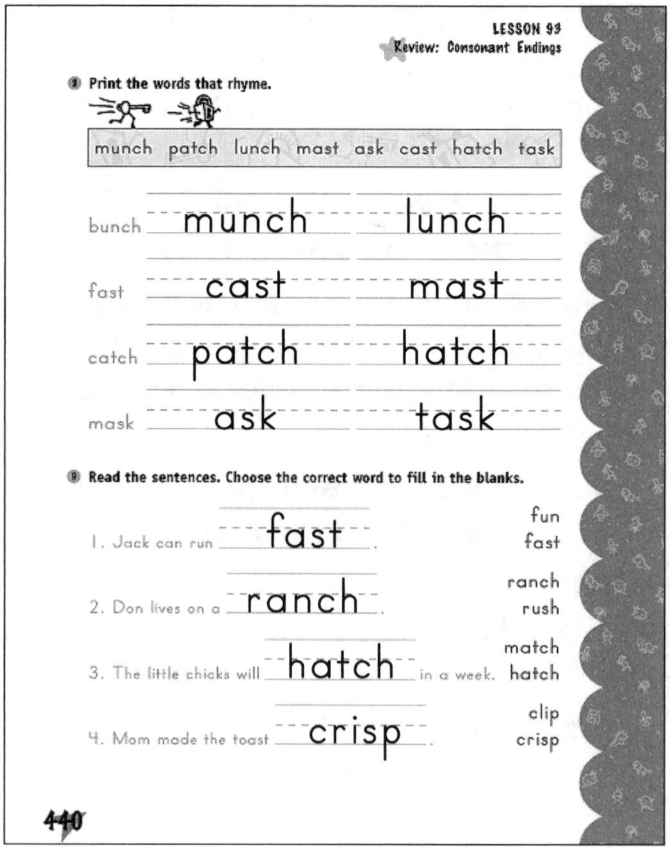

LESSON 93
Review: Consonant Endings

Print the words that rhyme.

| munch | patch | lunch | mast | ask | cast | hatch | task |

bunch   munch   lunch
fast   cast   mast
catch   patch   hatch
mask   ask   task

Read the sentences. Choose the correct word to fill in the blanks.

1. Jack can run   fast .   fun / fast
2. Don lives on a   ranch .   ranch / rush
3. The little chicks will   hatch   in a week.   match / hatch
4. Mom made the toast   crisp .   clip / crisp

440

Lesson 94 - Beginning Consonant Blends: tw, sw

Overview:

- Introduce beginning consonant blends **tw, sw**
- Yes / No sentences
- Spelling

Materials and Supplies:

- Teacher's Guide & Student Workbook
- White board
- Reader 3: *Twirls and Swirls*

Teaching Tips:

Use the white board in introducing the beginning blends **tw** and **sw** with other ending parts of words. Present the sound **tw** at the beginning of the word as in **twins**. Present the sound of **sw** at the beginning of the word as in **swing**.

Activity 1. Study the pictures and words together. Have the student choose and circle the blend that is heard at the beginning of each word.

Pictures: **sw**im, **sw**ept, **tw**ist, **st**eps
         sleep, **sw**itch, **tw**ig, **tw**ins

Activity 2. Print the words you have circled that start with the blends **sw** and **tw** on the lines below.

sw: **swim, swept, switch**
tw: **twist, twig, twins**

Activity 3. Read the make-up words.

Make-up Words: **stig, twam, stel, twif**

Activity 4. Read the puzzle sentences together. Have the student draw a line from the puzzle sentence to the picture it matches.

Pictures: **Jack can swim on a duck.**
The twins will swing on a dress.
Tom swept the twig.

Activity 5. Read the sentences. Put a circle around the **yes** if the statement is true or could happen. Circle **no** if the statement is not true or could not happen.

Her hand will swell when it is smashed. (**yes**)
You can swim when you stand up. (**no**)
It is fun to play on a swing. (**yes**)
All boys and girls are twins. (**no**)

Activity 6. Read the sentences and words together. Study the pictures. Have the student choose the word from the word bank that tells about the picture.

1. Ben will (**swim**) across the lake.
2. The boys and girls can have fun on the (**swing**).
3. Meg and Greg are (**twins**).
4. The train on the rail is (**swift**).

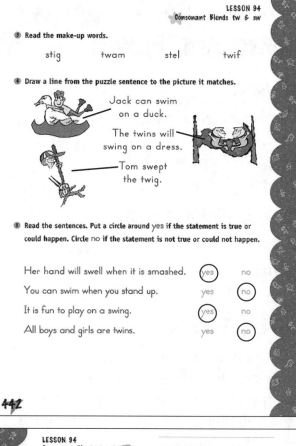

Activity 7. Spell the words under the pictures by filling in the beginning sounds you hear.

Pictures: **sw**ing, **tw**ins, **sw**ept
twig, **sw**ift, **sw**itch

Activity 8. Print the sentence on the lines below.

Sentence: **I like to swing on a swing.**

LESSON 94
Consonant Blends tw & sw

7 **Spell the words under the pictures by filling in the beginning sounds you hear.**

sw ing tw ins sw ept

tw ig sw ift sw itch

8 **Print the sentence.**

I like to swing on a swing.

444

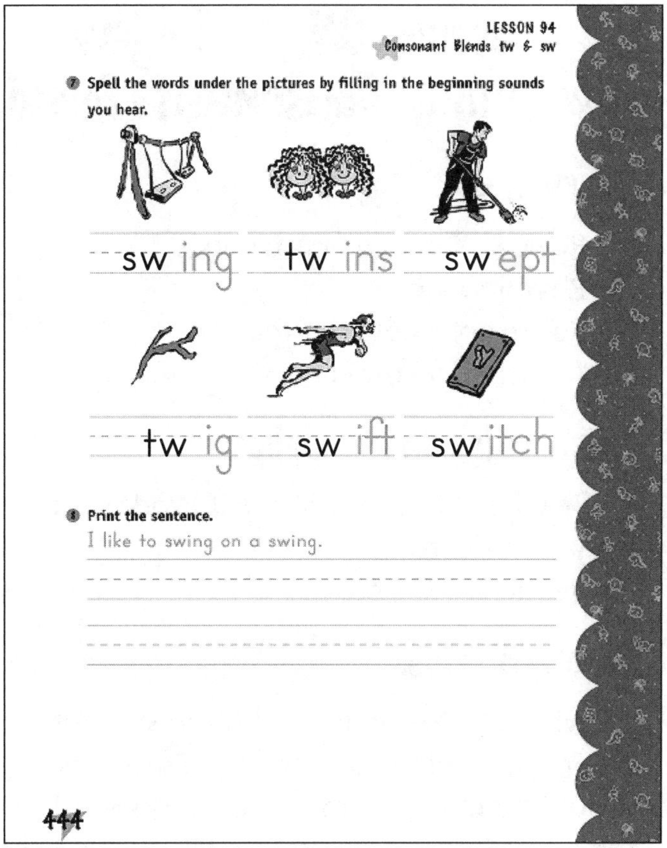

Lesson 95 - Review
Beginning Consonant Blends

Overview:

- Review of consonant blends
- Rhyming words
- Review of quotation marks
- Alphabetical order

Materials and Supplies:

- Teacher's Guide & Student Workbook
- White board
- Reader 3: *The Storm*

Teaching Tips:

Review all the pictures with the students before beginning each activity. Emphasis should be made on the beginning sounds. Use the white board to assist in review any of the words in question.

Activity 1. Study the pictures and discuss beginning blends. Have the student choose the correct beginning consonant blend for the pictures below.

Pictures: **tw**ins, **spr**inkle, **spr**ay, **st**ep
spring, **tw**ig, **st**ing, **spl**ash
spin, **qu**een, **spl**int, **tr**ip
snail, **sp**ell, **tw**ist, **sk**unk

Activity 2. Read one word from each of the boxes and have the student put a circle around the correct word in each box.

Words: **twin, twist, tweet**
step, stiff, staff
sprig, spring, spruce
slash, splash, sting
quilt, quit, quiz
spin, speed, spank

Activity 3. Read the words in the word box and sentences together. Have the student choose the correct word from the word bank to fill in the blanks.

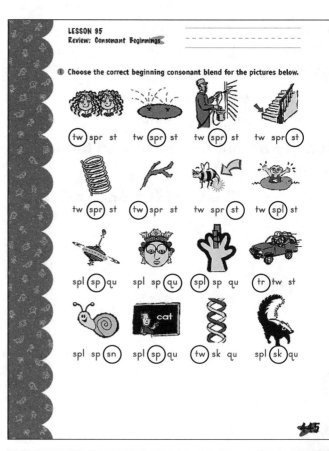

1. Dad will (**spray**) the paint.
2. Jed and Ted are (**twin**) boys.
3. I can (**step**) on rocks.
4. Beth has a top that can (**spin**).

Horizons Kindergarten Phonics

Activity 4. Print the words that rhyme.

twin/**spin, thin**
splash/**crash, trash**
spray/**tray, pray**
quit/**flit, sit**

Activity 5. Read the sentences. Put a circle around the **yes** if the statement is true or could happen. Circle **no** if the statement is not true or could not happen.

Bob is ten years old. Jeff is six. They are twins. (**no**)
Ben and Jeff went to splash in the mud. They are clean. (**no**)
Beth and Meg drink milk. They had a good lunch. (**yes**)
The queen sat on a soft bench. She was happy with her staff. (**yes**)

Activity 6. Spell the words under the pictures by printing the beginning blend sound.

Pictures: **qu**een, **spl**ash, **spr**ay
   spill, **qu**it, **spl**int

Activity 7. Print each set of words in alphabetical order.

Words: **quiz, spin, twist**
   mint, prize, sprint

Activity 8. Print the words in alphabetical order.

  Words: **dash, gift, speak**

Activity 9. Read the sets of sentences below. Discuss the pictures and their meanings. Have the student underline the correct sentence to match the picture.

  Sean will catch the ball.
  Sean will hatch the ball.

  The clasp will sting you.
  The wasp will sting you.

  Frank can run fast on the path.
  Frank can run much on the path.

Activity 10. Review placement of quotation marks. Have the student put quotation marks around the words that show someone is talking.

  1. Jack said, ["]I like to swim.["]
  2. ["]Please come here["], said the queen.
  3. ["]What time is it?["] asked Clay.

LESSON 95
Review: Consonant Beginnings

⑧ Print the words in alphabetical order.

gift   dash   speak

1. dash   2. gift   3. speak

⑨ Look at the sentences below. Underline the correct sentence to match the picture.

Sean will catch the ball.
Sean will hatch the ball.

The clasp will sting you.
The wasp will sting you.

Frank can run fast on the path.
Frank can run much on the path.

449

LESSON 95
Review: Consonant Beginnings

⑩ Print the following sentences. Put quotation marks around the words that show someone is talking.

Jack said, I like to swim.

Jack said, "I like to swim"

Please come here, said the queen.

"Please come here,"

said the queen.

What time is it? asked Clay.

"What time is it?" asked

Clay.

450

Lesson 96 - Review Ending Consonant Blends

Overview:

- Review of ending consonant blends
- Spelling
- Sentence comprehension
- Alphabetical order
- Ending blends identification
- Vocabulary development

Materials and Supplies:

- Teacher's Guide & Student Workbook
- White board
- Reader 3: *What's the Secret?*

Teaching Tips:

Review all the pictures with the student before beginning each activity. Emphasis should be made on the ending sounds. Use the white board to assist in review any of the words in question.

Activity 1. Study the pictures together and discuss the meaning of each for vocabulary development. Have the student choose the correct ending consonant blend for the pictures below.

Pictures: **shelf, bank, lift**
sink, hang, skunk
milk, mask, dish
scalp, desk, bush

Activity 2. Read the sentences and the words in the word bank together. Have the student choose the correct word from the word bank to fill the blanks.

1. I put my caps on a (**shelf**).
2. Jan's dress is made of (**silk**) cloth.
3. Mom put the dish in the (**sink**).
4. Fred saw a (**skunk**) on the road.
5. Jan said, "I like to drink (**milk**)."
6. The green (**bush**) has one more leaf.

Activity 3. Spell the words under the pictures by filling in the ending blends.

Pictures: sku**nk**, de**sk**, di**sh**

he**lp**, ri**ng**, ba**nk**

dri**nk**, mi**lk**, le**ft**

ma**sk**, sa**nk**, chi**ck**

Activity 4. Read the sentences together and discuss their meaning. Have the student put a circle around **could be** if the statement could happen. Put a circle around **no way** if it is something you would not want to happen.

I want to have a skunk in my bed. (**no way**)

Jack wants a glass of milk. (**could be**)

Jan has a dish in her ear. (**no way**)

The shelf has lots of hats. (**could be**)

I like to help my dad. (**could be**)

Activity 5. Print these words in alphabetical order.

Words: **apple, fish, left, spin**

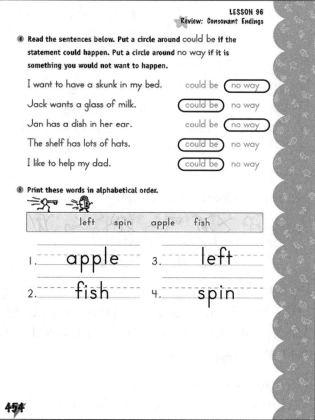

Activity 6. Study the ending blends of the words together. The words will not necessarily rhyme, but must have the same ending blends. Have the student print the words that have the same ending blends in a row.

Words: lf   **shelf, elf**
       ft   **raft, drift**
      ng   **sang, fang**
      nk   **sank, think**
      sk   **mask, flask**
      lk   **milk, silk**

Activity 7. Read the sentences together. Have the student print the vocabulary word that describes the sentence from the words in the word bank.

1. An animal that stinks is in the bush. (**skunk**)
2. A soft kind of cloth used to make a dress. (**silk**)
3. The teeth are very sharp. (**fang**)
4. When you use your brain, you do this. (**think**)
5. A little person in make-up stories. (**elf**)

LESSON 96
Review: Consonant Endings

⑥ Print the words that have the same ending blends in a row.

shelf	think	mask	raft	drift	milk
flask	sang	fang	elf	sank	silk

lf   shelf   elf

ft   raft   drift

ng   sang   fang

nk   sank   think

sk   mask   flask

lk   milk   silk

455

LESSON 96
Review: Consonant Endings

⑦ Read the sentences with your teacher. From the words in the word bank, print the vocabulary word that describes the sentence.

skunk	fang	think	silk	elf	milk

1. An animal that stinks is in the bush.   skunk

2. A soft kind of cloth used to make a dress.   silk

3. The teeth are very sharp.   fang

4. When you use your brain, you do this.   think

5. Something white to drink.   milk

6. A little person in make-up stories.   elf

456

Lesson 97 - Vowel Plus R: ar

Overview:

- Introduce vowel plus **r** – **ar**
- Rhyming words
- Introduce word search puzzle
- Vocabulary development

Materials and Supplies:

- Teacher's Guide & Student Workbook
- White board
- Reader 3: *Barb's Scarf*

Teaching Tips:

Introduction of the Vowel Plus **R** Rule: When a word has **ar** in it, it makes the sound we hear in **car**. It can be used at the beginning of a word as in **arch**, or in the middle of the word as in **market**.

Activity 1. Study the pictures and words together. Emphasize the placement and sound of **ar**. Have the student put a circle around the pictures that have the sound of **ar** in them.

Pictures: **cart, spring, car, barn
star, fast, market, farm**

Activity 2. Practice printing words with **ar** in them. Underline the **ar** in each word.

Pictures: **star, part, bar
spark, arm, market**

Activity 3. Read the sentences together. Have the student draw a line from the picture to match the sentence. Underline the words that have **ar** in them.

Pictures: **The shark has sharp teeth.
We saw a spark from the fire.
Carl and I like to ride in a cart.
Dar had a party for the kids.**

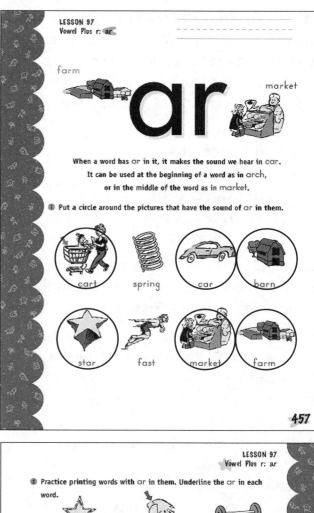

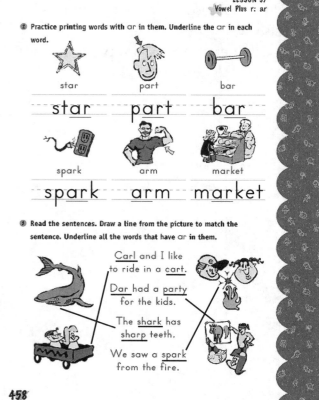

Activity 4. Read the words together. Have the student print the words on the lines below that rhyme with the word bank.

car/**far, Dar, jar**
dark/**mark, lark, shark**
card/**chard, hard, lard**
arm/**charm, harm, farm**

Activity 5. Read the make-up words.

Make-up Words: **kark, chark, gark, jark**

Activity 6. Read the puzzle phrases together and study the pictures. Have the student draw a line from the puzzle phrase to the picture it matches.

Pictures: **a dog with an arm**
   a farm on a jar
   a car on a barn
   a shark in the cat dish

Activity 7. Illustrate the word search puzzle. Read the words going across and down with the student. Have him circle the words that go in each direction, explaining that some of the letters will overlap.

Words Across: **park, shark, farm**
Words Down: **dark, arm, star**

Lesson 98 - Vowel Plus r: or

Overview:

- Introduce vowel plus **r** – **or**
- Capitalization and punctuation
- Vocabulary words in sentences

Materials and Supplies:

- Teacher's Guide & Student Workbook
- White board
- Reader 3: *Stork*

Teaching Tips:

Introduction of the Vowel Plus **R** Rule: When a word has **or** in it, the **or** makes the sound we hear in the middle of **corn**. It can be used at the beginning of a word as in **order**, or at the end of the word as in **for**.

Activity 1. Study the pictures and words together. Have the student put a circle around the pictures that have the sound of **or** in them.

Pictures: **fork, shore, cork, stork**
horse, horn, thorn, orchard

Activity 2. Practice printing words with **or** in them. Underline the **or** in each word.

Pictures: **horn, sport, fork**
shore, thorn, dorm

Activity 3. Read the sentences together. Have the student draw a line from the picture to match the sentence. Underline all the words that have **or** in them.

Pictures: **Put the fork by the plate.**
The rose has thorns on the stem.
Bob rode the horse to the barn.
Norm has a torch in his hand.

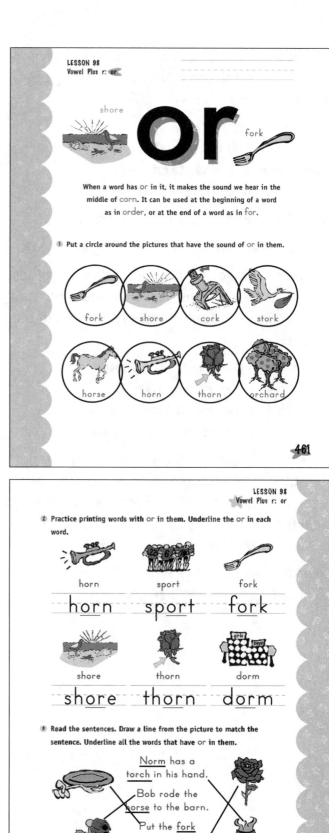

Horizons Kindergarten Phonics

Activity 4. Read the puzzle phrase together. Have the student draw a line from the puzzle phrase to the picture it matches.

Pictures: **a cord on a fork**
a horn in a storm
a short stork
a cork on a thorn

Activity 5. Read the make-up words.

Make-up Words: **corb, stort, dort, lorf**

Activity 6. Review using a capital letter at the beginning of a sentence and a period or question mark at the end. Have the student print the sentences below.

The thorn was sharp**.**
Did the man honk the horn on the car**?**

Activity 7. Read the sentences and words together. Discuss the vocabulary words and meanings. Have the student choose the vocabulary word that describes the sentence and then print it on the line below.

1. The alarm clock rings first thing in the day. (**morning**)
2. The roses have sharp points on the stems. (**thorns**)
3. Many people live there and go to school. (**dorm**)
4. A bird that has long legs and can fly fast. (**stork**)
5. This is put in the top of a bottle. (**cork**)
6. This is what we call the meat from a pig. (**pork**)
7. Fruit trees are planted together. (**orchard**)

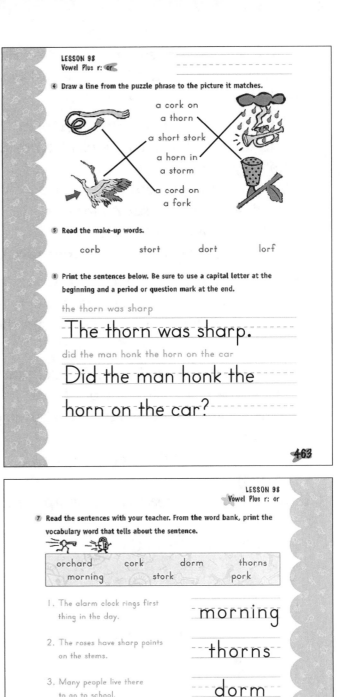

Activity 8. Read the sentences together. Have the student choose and print the correct word from the word bank on the blanks.

1. The tree fell down in a strong (**storm**).
2. The sun may (**scorch**) the plant on this hot day.
3. We put a short (**cord**) on the cart.
4. Football is a good (**sport**) for kids.
5. Did you (**sort**) out the (**forks**)?
6. Apple trees are planted in an (**orchard**).

Activity 9. Read the sentences and words in the word bank together. Have the student print the vocabulary word that tells about the picture.

1. A wagon that could be big or little. (**cart**)
2. Place where animals are kept. (**barn**)
3. A place where you could see a big building. (**farm**)
4. You have two of these on your body. (**arms**)
5. A big fish in the sea that has sharp teeth. (**shark**)
6. A place to put food. (**jar**)

LESSON 98
Vowel Plus r: or

Read the sentences. Choose the correct word from the word bank and print it in the blanks.

| orchard | cord | storm | sport |
| sort | | scorch | forks |

1. The tree fell down in a strong __storm__
2. The sun may __scorch__ the plant on this hot day.
3. We put a short __cord__ on the cart.
4. Football is a good __sport__ for kids.
5. Did you __sort__ out the __forks__ ?
6. Apple trees are planted in an __orchard__

465

LESSON 98
Vowel Plus r: or

Read the sentences with your teacher. From the words in the word bank, print the vocabulary word that tells about the sentence.

| barn | arms | farm | shark | cart | jar |

1. A wagon that could be big or little. __cart__
2. Place where animals are kept. __barn__
3. A place where you could see a big building. __farm__
4. You have two of these on your body. __arms__
5. A big fish in the sea that has sharp teeth. __shark__
6. A place to put food. __jar__

466

Lesson 99 - Review
Vowel Plus R: ar, or

Overview:

- Review vowel plus **r** – **ar, or**
- Alphabetical order
- Vocabulary words in sentences

Materials and Supplies:

- Teacher's Guide & Student Workbook
- White board
- Reader 3: *Where are the Sharks?*

Teaching Tips:

Review the rule for Vowel Plus **R** - **ar** and **or**. Use the white board to assist in reviewing any of the words in question.

Activity 1. Study the pictures and discuss the meaning for vocabulary development. Have the student choose the correct vowel plus **r** for the sound you hear in the pictures.

Pictures: c**ar**t, st**or**e, th**or**n, f**ar**m
b**ar**n, c**or**k, sp**or**t, c**ar**d

Activity 2. Print the words below the pictures. Put a circle around the words that have **ar** in them. Underline the words that have **or** in them.

ar: **dart, shark, spark, sharp**
or: **corn, horse, stork, thorn, north**

Activity 3. Read the sentences and words in the word bank together. Have the student choose the correct word from the word bank to fill in the blanks.

1. There was a (**spark**) from the fire.
2. The boys and girls can ride the (**horse**).
3. Mom had (**torn**) her dress.
4. The (**lark**) sang a pretty song.
5. Dad had a (**horn**) on his truck to toot.
6. Carl sent a birthday (**card**) to Norm.

Activity 4. Read one word from each of the boxes and have the student put a circle around the correct word in each box.

Words: **cart, barn, fort**
born, charm, shark
farm, sport, pork
horse, dart, jar

Activity 5. Spell the words under the pictures with **or** or **ar**.

Words: st**or**k, c**or**k, c**ar**d, f**or**t, sp**or**t, f**or**k

Activity 6. Read the sentences together. Have the student put a circle around **yes** if the statement could happen. Put a circle around **no** if it is something you would not want to happen.

1. The sharks swim in the sea. (**could be**)
2. We ate lunch with a cork. (**no way**)
3. It is fun to live on a farm. (**could be**)
4. Dan and Jim had a good card game.
   (**could be**)
5. We will park the car in the barn. (**no way**)
6. We eat pork that comes from a rat.
   (**no way**)

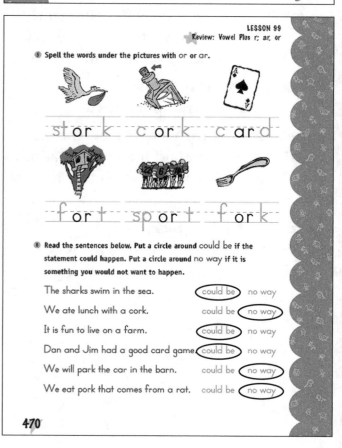

Activity 7. Read the sentences and the words in the word bank together. Have the student print the vocabulary word that tells about the picture.

1. Men use a brush to paint pictures. (**art**)
2. We like to ride this animal. (**horse**)
3. A sharp point on a rose can hurt you. (**thorn**)
4. Do not use too hot an iron to press your dress. (**scorch**)
5. A farm building that is a good place for animals. (**barn**)

Activity 8. Put the words in alphabetical order.

Words: **born, card, dark**
        barn, horse, pork

Activity 9. Color the picture.

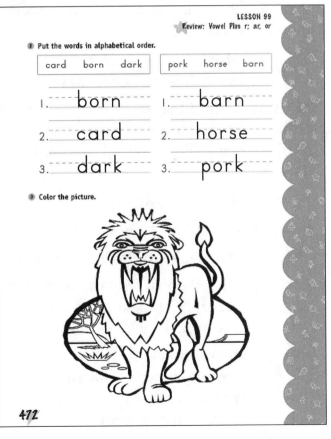

Lesson 100 - Review
Vowel Plus R: ar

Overview:

- Review vowel plus **r** – **ar**
- Vocabulary Words in sentences

Materials and Supplies:

- Teacher's Guide & Student Workbook
- White board
- Reader 3: *Carl and the Farm*

Teaching Tips:

Review the rule for Vowel Plus **r** - **ar**. Use the white board to assist in reviewing any of the words in question.

Activity 1. Study the pictures together. Have the student put a circle around the pictures that have the sound of **ar** in them. Underline the **ar** in each word.

Pictures: **dart, jar, park, catch
star, brush, yarn, march**

Activity 2. Read the words in the word bank. Choose and spell the correct word under each picture. Then print the rest of the words on the lines.

Pictures: **barn, shark, star**

Activity 3. Read the make-up words.

Make-up Words: **karb, jarb, darf, slark**

Activity 4. Read one word from each of the boxes and have the student put a circle around the correct word in each box.

Words: **alarm, mark, hark
market, marsh, charm
star, cart, farm
mart, darn, marsh**

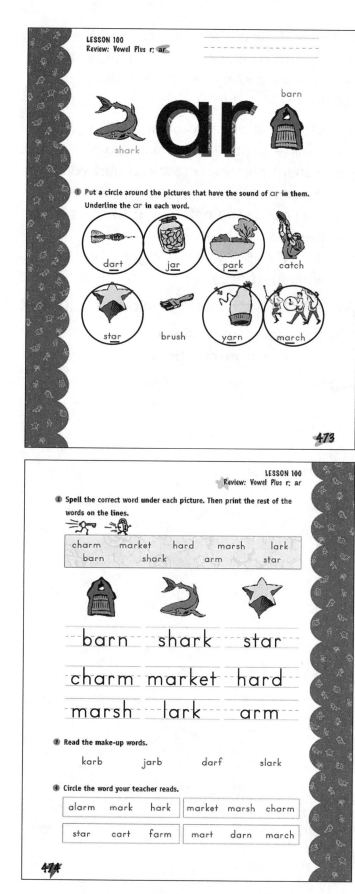

Activity 5. Read the sentences and word choices together. Have the student choose and print the correct word to finish each sentence.

    1. We rode to the barn in a (**cart**).
    2. Mark saw a (**star**) in the sky.
    3. The (**alarm**) clock was set for six.
    4. The big dog will (**bark**) at the cars.
    5. The horse lives on a (**farm**).
    6. Mom will buy food at the (**market**).

Activity 6. Read the sentences together and study the pictures. Have the student draw a line from the picture to match the sentence. Underline all the words that have **ar** in them.

    Pictures:
    We can play on the bars in the park.
    Ted's dog, Spot, will bark at the cats.
    The horse will trot to the barn.
    Tom is a short boy.

Activity 7. Read the puzzle phrases together. Have the student draw a line from the puzzle phrase to the picture it matches.

    Pictures: **a card in a jar**
                a star on his arm
                a park on a cart
                a shark on a chart

Activity 8. Read the sentences and words in the word bank together. Have the student choose the vocabulary word from the word bank that describes the sentence. Print the words in the blanks.

    1. You can put things in this glass (**jar**).
    2. We played a game and had some (**cards**).
    3. Clark put the horses in a barn on the (**farm**).
    4. You use your brain and are very (**smart**).
    5. The teacher put a note on a (**chart**).

Lesson 101 - Vowel Plus R: or

Overview:
- Review vowel plus **r** – **or**
- Crossword puzzle
- Vocabulary words in sentences

Materials and Supplies:
- Teacher's Guide & Student Workbook
- White board
- Reader 3: *The Fishing Trip*

Teaching Tips:

Review the rule for Vowel Plus **r** – **or**. Use the white board to assist in reviewing any of the words in question.

Activity 1. Study the pictures and words together. Have the student put a circle around the pictures that have the sound of **or** in them. Underline the **or** in each word.

Pictures: **corn, park, cord, skunk storm, horse, porch, stork**

Activities 2 & 3. Spell the correct word below each picture. Then print the words from the word bank on the lines.

Pictures: **stork, fork, corn, horn**

Words: **sport, thorn, dorm, shore, more, cork**

Activity 4. Put a circle around the words you find in the puzzle. The words will go across and down.

Across: **cord, market, torn, dorm, sort**
Down: **pork, dart, horse, morn**

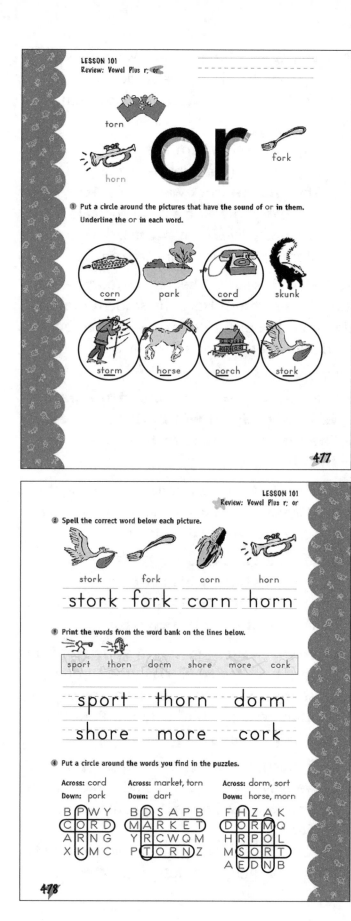

Activity 5. Read the sentences and words together. Have the student choose the correct word to finish each sentence and print it in the blank.

1. A wind (**storm**) broke the branch.
2. Mom can fix a lunch with (**corn**).
3. We saw the long legs on the (**stork**).
4. For dinner, we had a (**pork**) roast.
5. The rose plant has a sharp (**thorn**).
6. Dad put a (**cork**) in the bottle.
7. We ate some cake and wanted (**more**).

Activity 6. Read one word from each of the boxes and have the student put a circle around the correct word in each box.

Words: **fort, short, pork**
      north, dorm, fork
      cork, sworn, more
      horn, cord, corn

Activity 7. Read the sentences. Put a circle around the **yes** if the statement is true or could happen. Circle **no** if the statement is not true or could not happen.

1. I think cork is good to eat. (**no**)
2. It is good to have a horse to ride. (**yes**)
3. We need to live in a storm. (**no**)
4. We will ride in a cart more than 300 miles. (**yes**)
5. The thorn from a rose is what I want in my hand. (**no**)
6. It is fun to do artwork. (**yes**)

Activity 8. Print the words in alphabetical order.

Words: **dorm, horn, more, short**
      cork, Ford, north, sort

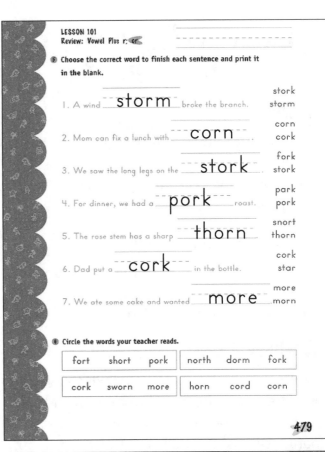

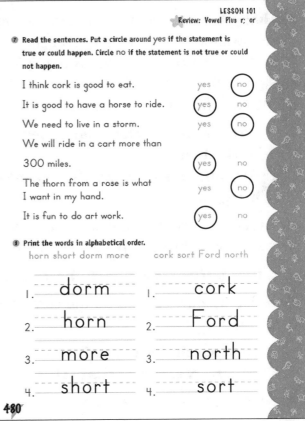

Lesson 102 - Vowel Plus R: er, ir, ur

Overview:

- Introduce vowel plus **r** – with emphasis on **er**
- Vocabulary words in sentences
- Spelling

Materials and Supplies:

- Teacher's Guide & Student Workbook
- White board
- Reader 3: *Bird Watching*

Teaching Tips:

Introduce the rule for Vowel Plus **r** – **er**, **ir**, **ur**. Use the white board to demonstrate **er** with various beginning and ending consonants. Discuss meanings of the words.

Activity 1. Have the student read the words, being aware of the Vowel Plus **r** in each one. Put a CIRCLE around the words that are spelled with **er**. UNDERLINE the **ir** words. Put a SQUARE around the **ur** words.

er: **swerve, verse, clerk, jerk, her**
ir: **bird, shirt**
ur: **fur, nurse, surf, bur, church, blur, burg, spur**

Activity 2. Circle all the words that have the **er** sound as in **her** and have **er** in them.

er: **perch, fern, Bert, jerk, herd, serve**

Activity 3. Practice printing the correct word below each picture.

Pictures: **perch, Bert, herd, berth nerve, serve, Gert, stern**

Activity 4. Read the make-up words.

Make-up Words: **terb, derp, ler, jerj**

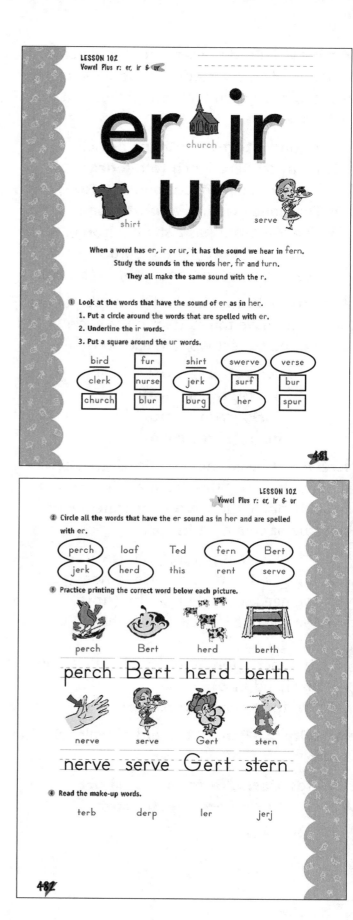

Activity 5. Read the sentences together. Have the student draw a line from the picture to match the sentence. Underline all the words that have an **er** sound in them and are spelled with the letters **er**.

Pictures: **A rope could jerk from your hands.**
The green fern is a plant.
A herd of cattle ate the grass.

Activity 6. Read the sentences together. Have the student put a circle around **could be** if it is true or something that could happen. Put a circle around **no way** if it is not true or could not happen.

Kirk can put on his shirt. (**could be**)
All boys like to wear blue skirts. (**no way**)
I learned the third verse from the Bible.
(**could be**)
It is fun to twirl a rope. (**could be**)
I am thirty years old today. (**no way**)

Activity 7. Read the sentences and words together. Have the student choose and print the vocabulary word from the word bank that tells about the picture.

1. Merv went to see a group of cattle.
   (**herd**)
2. Bert should read a part of the Bible.
   (**verse**)
3. The clerk looks cross and has no smile.
   (**stern**)
4. The coat belongs to the girl. (**hers**)

Activity 8. Look at the words that end with the letters **er**. Underline the **er** in each word.

Words: **mother, sister, brother, butter, banker, camper, hunter, singer**

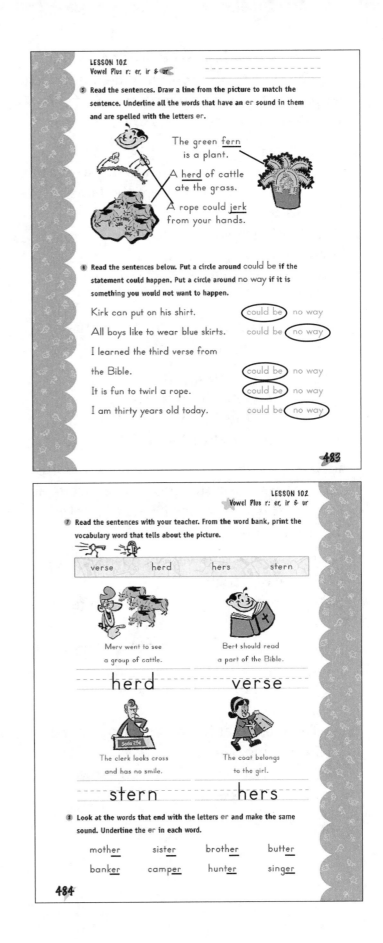

Activity 9. Read the sentences below. Put a circle around **could be** if the statement could happen. Put a circle around **no way** if it is something you would not want to happen.

Bert should jerk her arm. (**no way**)
All horses like to perch in a tree. (**no way**)
I like to learn the verse from the Bible.
(**could be**)
The herd of sheep likes to live on a boat.
(**no way**)
There are many herbs you can eat.
(**could be**)

Activity 10. Draw a line from the puzzle phrase to the picture it matches.

Pictures: **corn on a perch**
swerve into a stump
a dog in a fern
a cat that jerks

Activity 11. Read the sentences and words together. Have the student choose the vocabulary word from the word bank that tells about the sentence.

1. A big white bird with long legs was on the lake. (**stork**)
2. I got out of bed when the alarm rang early. (**morning**)
3. Mark has a coat that is not as long as he wants it. (**short**)
4. We put a top in the bottle so it would not spill. (**cork**)
5. The meat that Mom fixed for dinner came from a pig. (**pork**)
6. The string was put on a lamp so we could turn it on. (**cord**)

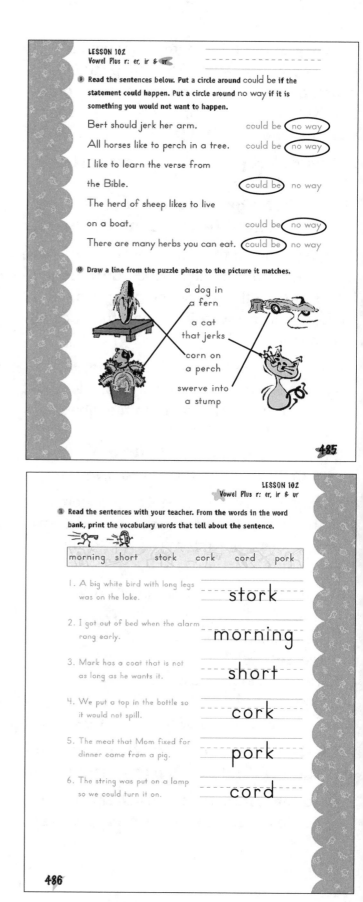

Lesson 103 - Vowel Plus R: ir

Overview:

- Review vowel plus **r** – with emphasis on **ir**
- Vocabulary words in sentences
- Spelling

Materials and Supplies:

- Teacher's Guide & Student Workbook
- White board
- Reader 3: *The Birthday Trade*

Teaching Tips:

Review the rule for Vowel Plus **r**. Emphasize words using **ir** in them. Use the white board to demonstrate **ir** with various beginning and ending consonants. Discuss meaning of the words.

Activity 1. Review the Vowel Plus **r** again. Have the students read the words, being aware of the spelling of each. Student will put a CIRCLE around the words that are spelled with **ir**. UNDERLINE the **er** words. Put a SQUARE around the **ur** words.

   ir: **bird, fir, shirt, quirk, dirt,**
       firm, birth, skirt
   er: **nerve, verse, perk, hers**
   ur: **turf, church, purr**

Activity 2. Read the words together. Have the student circle all the words that have the **ir** sound as in **bird** and are spelled with **ir**.

   ir: **squirt, thirst, birth, stir,**
      shirt, Dirk, flirt, smirk

Activity 3. Practice printing the correct word below each picture.

   Pictures: **bird, third, dirt, chirp**
           smirk, whirl, first, fir

Activity 4. Read the make-up words.

   Make-up Words: **birb, dirp, mib, jirj**

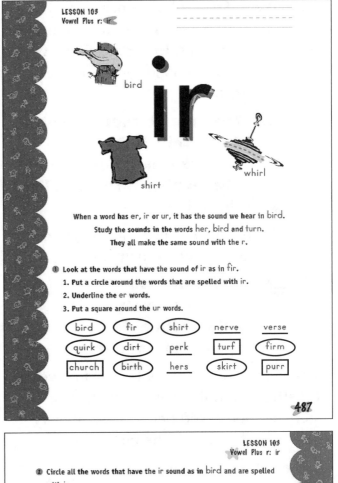

Activity 5. Read the sentences together. Have the student draw a line from the picture to match the sentence. Underline all the words that have an **ir** sound in them and are spelled with the letters **ir**.

Pictures: **The green fern is a plant.**
Gert's skirt is green.
A smirk is not a good smile.
The number three is called the third one.

Activity 6. Draw a line from the puzzle phrase to the picture it matches.

Pictures: **a bird in a whirl**
dirt on a porch
a dog with a skirt
a cat who has a shirt

Activity 7. Read the sentences and words together. From the word bank, have the student choose and print the vocabulary word that tells about the picture.

The hat is hers. (**girl**)
The feathers of this little one are yellow. (**bird**)
Mom told her three times. (**third**)
The smile is not a nice one. (**smirk**)

Activity 8. Read one word from each of the boxes and have the student put a circle around the correct word in each box.

Words: **bird, shirt, fern**
birch, first, third
cart, birth, skirt
chirp, sir, dirt

Lesson 104 - Vowel Plus R: ur

Overview:

- Review vowel plus **r** with emphasis on **ur**
- Vocabulary words in sentences
- Spelling

Materials and Supplies:

- Teacher's Guide & Student Workbook
- White board
- Reader 3: *Herb's Camping Trip*

Teaching Tips:

Review the rule for Vowel Plus **r**. Emphasize words using **ur** in them. Use the white board to demonstrate **ur** with various beginning and ending consonants. Discuss meaning of the words.

Activity 1. Review the Vowel Plus **r** again. Have the students read the words, being aware of the spelling of each. Student will put a CIRCLE around the words that are spelled with **ur**. UNDERLINE the **ir** words. Put a SQUARE around the **er** words.

ur: **purse, fur, nurse, surf, Turk, bur,
burn, curl, hurl, church, burst**

ir: **shirt, shirk**

er: **clerk, jerk**

Activity 2. Circle all the words that have the **ur** sound as in **burn** and have **ur** in them.

ur: **turn, surf, churn
curse, purse, curl**

Activity 3. Practice printing the correct word below each picture.

Pictures: **spur, purple, turkey, curve
purse, Curt, fur, curb**

Activity 4. Read the make-up words.

Make-up Words: **furb, gurp, murd, kurf**

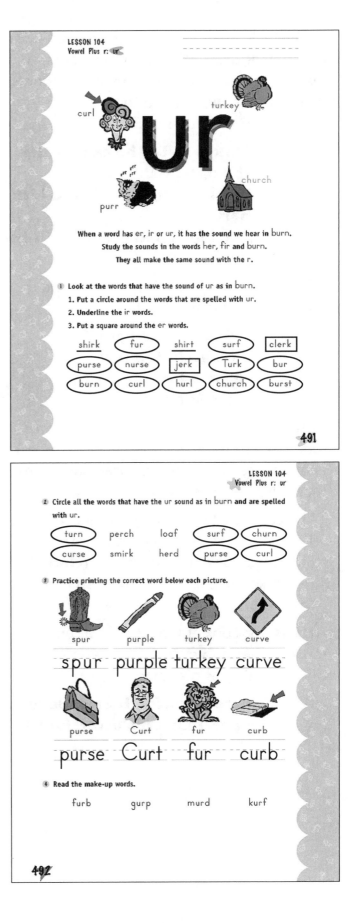

Activity 5. Read the sentences together. Have the student draw a line from the picture to match the sentence. Underline all the words that have the **ur** sound in them and are spelled with the letters **ur**.

Pictures: **Turk is so big he can hurdle the gate.**
The ball can burst if you kick it hard.
The nurse had her hand in her purse.

Activity 6. Draw a line from the puzzle phrase to the picture it matches.

Pictures: **a dog who can purr**
a churn in the surf
fir on a bird
a cat in a purse

Activity 7. Read the sentences and words together. From the word bank, have the student choose and print the vocabulary word that tells about the picture.

The cub's coat is black and white. (**fur**)
The kitten tells us he is happy. (**purr**)
Butter has to whirl to be made. (**churn**)
He broke the ball by hitting it too hard. (**burst**)

Activity 8. Look at the words that end with the letters **er** and make the same sound. Underline the **er** in each word.

Words: **bumper, surfer, buster, duller upper, muster, bluster, junker**

Horizons Kindergarten Phonics

Lesson 105 - Review
Vowel Plus R: er, ir, ur

Overview:

- Review vowel plus **r**
- Sentence completion
- Rhyming

Materials and Supplies:

- Teacher's Guide & Student Workbook
- White board
- Reader 3: *Purt, the Kitten*

Teaching Tips:

Review the rule for Vowel plus **r** covering all the vowels. Discuss vocabulary words and their meanings.

Activity 1. Study the pictures together. Have the student put a circle around the words that have the same sound as the words **Bert**, **shirt**, or **surf**.

Words: **shark, cart, burn, burst twirl, short, bird, third**

Activity 2. Read the sentences and words together. Have the student choose and print the correct word to complete the sentence.

1. The green (**fern**) was on the porch.
2. We were the (**first**) ones in line.
3. The (**surf**) came over the shore.
4. The chick will (**perch**) on the gate.
5. The baby (**bird**) will chirp in the nest.
6. The (**nurse**) can help Turk take his pills.

Activity 3. Print the words that rhyme.

Kirk/**lurk, perk**
hurt/**Bert, flirt**
stir/**her, fur**

Activity 4. Practice printing the correct word below each picture.

Pictures: **shirt, herd, fern
church, purse, skirt**

Activity 5. Read the sentences together. Have the student draw a line from the picture to match the sentence. Underline all the words that have an **er**, **ir**, or **ur** sound in them.

Pictures: **We slept in the berth on the train.
The birch tree is big.
The bird will take a bath in the birdbath.
He hit a nerve in his hand and it hurt.**

Activity 6. Match the words from the word bank with the correct vowel plus sound and print the words in columns.

Words:
er	**ir**	**ur**
jerk	birth	fur
herd	squirt	lurch
perch	stir	
term	birch	

Activity 7. Read one word from each of the boxes and have the student put a circle around the correct word in each box.

Words: **bird, shirt, skirt
purr, fur, stir
herd, whirl, dirt
churn, burst, fern**

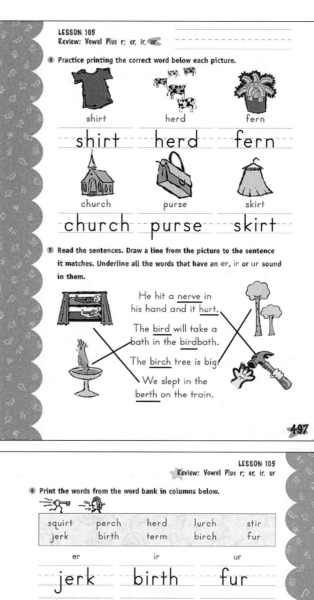

Activity 8. Read the sentences and words together. Have the student choose and print the correct word from the word bank to fill in the blanks.

1. Gert is a (**clerk**) at the store.
2. The pop will (**squirt**) all over us.
3. They told us about the (**birth**) of baby Jesus.
4. The boys put on their pants and (**shirts**).
5. The (**herd**) of goats liked the green grass.
6. The girl had a (**purse**) to hold her money.
7. The yellow (**bird**) made a nest in the birch tree.

Activity 9. Read the sentences together. Have the student put a circle around **could be** if the statement could happen. Put a circle around **no way** if it is something you would not want to happen.

The kitten hid under the porch. (**could be**)
The surf is too big so we can not swim. (**could be**)
Turk, my brother, has fur on his back. (**no way**)
Mom had to urge me to get up this morning. (**could be**)

Activity 10. The student will draw a picture and color it, then describe the picture.

---

⑧ Read the sentences. Choose the correct word from the word bank to fill in the blanks.

| birth | shirts | squirt | bird | purse | clerk | herd |

1. Gert is a _clerk_ at the store.
2. The soda pop will _squirt_ all over us.
3. They told us about the _birth_ of baby Jesus.
4. The boys put on their pants and _shirts_.
5. The _herd_ of goats liked the green grass.
6. The girl had a red _purse_ to hold her money.
7. The yellow _bird_ made a nest in the birch tree.

499

---

⑨ Read the sentences below. Put a circle around could be if the statement could happen. Put a circle around no way if it is something you would not want to happen.

The kitten hid under the porch. (could be) no way
The surf is too big so we cannot swim. (could be) no way
Turk, my brother, has fur on his back. could be (no way)
Mom had to urge me to get up this morning. (could be) no way

⑩ Draw a picture and color it. Tell your teacher about the picture.

500

Horizons Kindergarten Phonics

Lesson 106 - Review Vowel Plus R: ar, or

Overview:

- Review vowel plus **r** – **ar, or**
- Vocabulary words in sentences
- Words in columns

Materials and Supplies:

- Teacher's Guide & Student Workbook
- White board
- Reader 3: *Dirk's Bike Ride*

Teaching Tips:

Review the rule for Vowel plus **r** with emphasis on **ar** and **or**. Discuss vocabulary words and their meanings.

Activity 1. Study the pictures and words. Have the student put a circle around all the pictures that have the sound of **or** in them. Underline the **or** in each word.

Pictures: **sport, horse, thorn, cart farm, storm, dorm, cork**

Activity 2. Study the pictures and words. Have the student put a circle around all the pictures that have the sound of **ar** in them. Underline the **ar** in each word.

Pictures: **park, dart, stork, barn cord, shark, lark, spark**

Activity 3. Print the words in alphabetical order.

Words: **arch, lark, starch bar, carp, pork bark, porch, star**

Activity 4. Choose and print the correct word to complete the sentences.

1. Norm can paint the (**art**) for the chart.
2. The boat came to the (**shore**) of the lake.
3. When were you (**born**)?
4. Dan and Mike can be (**partners**).
5. Mom made a coat out of red (**yarn**).
6. The (**shark**) can bite.
7. A (**carp**) is a fish that swims in the lake.
8. Mark can (**snore**) when he sleeps.
9. We put the hens in the (**yard**).

Activity 5. Draw a line from the picture to the sentence it matches.

Pictures: **Barb rides a horse named Star.**
Merle puts a note on the chart.
Bert lives on a farm with sheep, horses, and goats.
Mom can darn my socks.
The baby was born in the barn.
The fire made a spark.

Activity 6. Read the sentences together. Have the student put a circle around **yes** if the statement is true or could happen. Circle **no** if the statement is not true or could not happen.

A lark is a pretty bird. (**yes**)
We can play in a park. (**yes**)
A star can sing all day. (**no**)
Corn is good to eat. (**yes**)

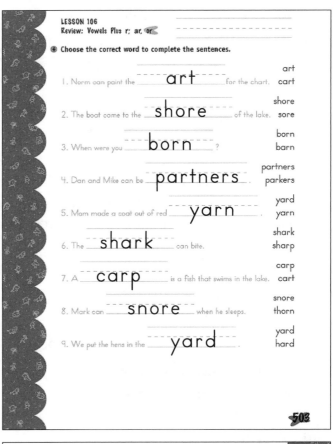

Activity 7. Print the words in columns.

Words:

ar:	or:
arch	porch
dart	corn
charm	more
scarf	score
start	scorch

Activity 8. Read the sentences together. Have the student put a circle around **yes** if the statement is true or could happen. Circle **no** if the statement is not true or could not happen.

It is fun to have a sore arm. (**no**)
A dog can purr. (**no**)
A horn must have a scarf. (**no**)

Activity 9. Print the words that rhyme.

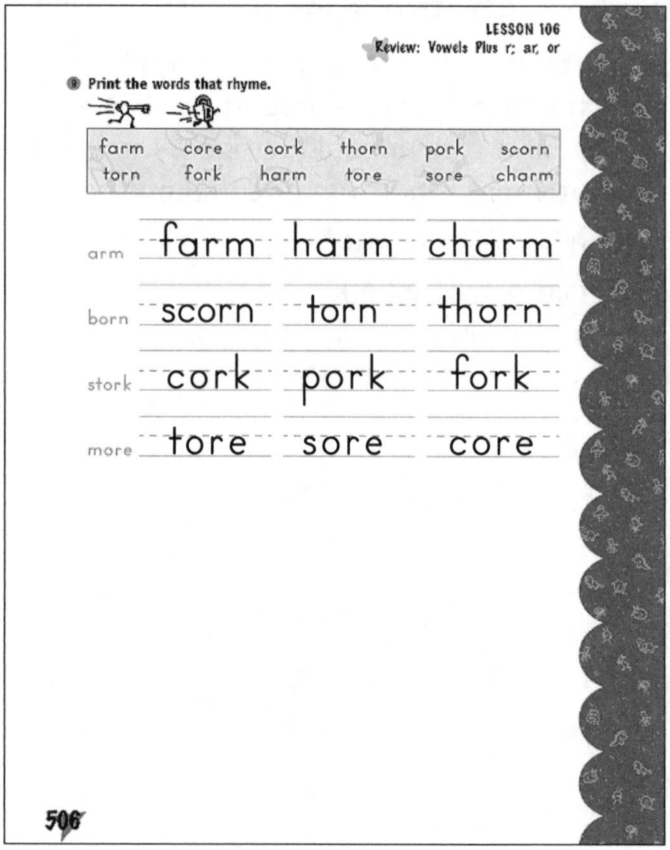

arm/**farm, harm, charm**
born/**scorn, torn, thorn**
stork/**cork, pork, fork**
more/**tore, sore, core**

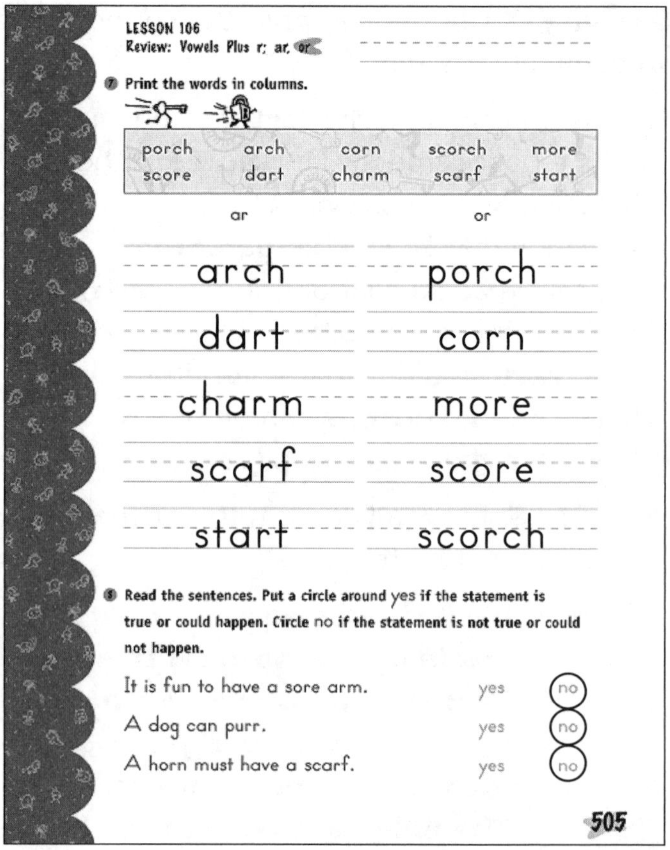

Lesson 107 - Review All Vowels Plus R

Overview:

- Review vowel plus **r** – all vowels
- Vocabulary words in sentences
- Rhyming
- Alphabetizing

Materials and Supplies:

- Teacher's Guide & Student Workbook
- White board
- Reader 3: *Gert's Painting*

Teaching Tips:

Review the rule for Vowel plus **r** using all the vowels. Use the white board as necessary for reviewing vocabulary words.

Activity 1. Study the pictures together. Have the student put a circle around the pictures that have the **er** sound as in **Gert**, **turf**, or **shirt**.

> Pictures: **skirt, car, bird, dirt**
> **smirk, churn, yard, fur**

Activity 2. Study the pictures together. Have the student put a circle around the pictures that have the **or** sound as in **born**.

> Pictures: **horn, barn, stork, corn**
> **short, scorch, start, porch**

Activity 3. Study the pictures together. Have the student put a circle around the pictures that have the **ar** sound as in **park**.

> Pictures: **bar, arm, shore, fern**
> **star, jar, scarf, shark**

Activity 4. Put the words in alphabetical order.

> Words: **farm, fork, stork**
> **arm, burst, car**

Activity 5. Read the sentences and words together. Have the student choose and print the correct word to complete the sentence.

1. The (**score**) of the game was 7 to 3.
2. We had to (**start**) the car.
3. Dad can (**honk**) his horn.
4. The nurse put the pills in her (**purse**).
5. The rider used his (**spur**) on the horse.
6. Barb (**wore**) her pretty dress to church.
7. All the goats were put in the (**barn**).

Activity 6. Discuss rhyming that must have the identical ending sound, but does not necessarily have the same spelling. Have the student print the words that rhyme.

bark/**lark, dark, park**
birch/**perch, church, lurch**
more/**core, chore, store**
turn/**burn, churn, fern**

Activity 7. Draw a line between the word and the picture it matches.

Pictures: **stork, purse, corn, fern, park, skirt**

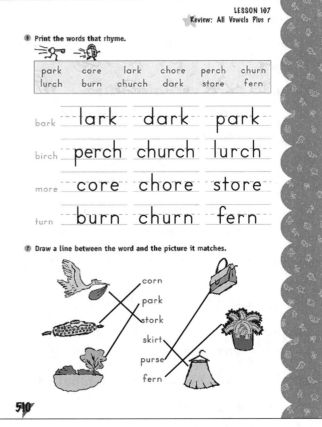

Lesson 108 - Plurals: Adding s

Overview:
- Introduce plurals – adding **s** for more than one
- Spelling

Materials and Supplies:
- Teacher's Guide & Student Workbook
- White board
- Reader 3: *The Full Trunk*

Teaching Tips:
Introduce plurals by using concrete objects for showing one. Discuss adding more and showing the additional object. Emphasize the final **s** so the sound is familiar.

Activity 1. Study the pictures and discuss the number of objects in each set. Indicate that having a number word is a clue to add an **s**, showing it is plural. Have the student put a circle around the pictures that show it is plural (or more than one in that picture).

> Pictures: **two cats, one bird, four birds**
> **three shirts, two birds, one shirt**
> **one table, three birds, four sticks**
> **two books, one horse, three dogs**

Activity 2. Spell the words under each picture. If there are more than one objects in the picture, print an **s** at the end of the word.

Pictures:		
I can	**2 cans**	
I cake	**3 cakes**	
I bat	**4 bats**	
1 hand	**2 hands**	
1 cap	**3 caps**	

Activity 3. Draw a line from the phrase to the picture it matches.

   Pictures: **three gifts, one duck,
   one frog, three pigs,
   five chicks, two sleds**

Activity 4. Choose and print the correct word to complete the sentence.

   1. Jack has two (**cats**) for pets.
   2. Mike saw three (**rats**) in the yard.
   3. One (**duck**) was near the lake.
   4. Three (**birds**) were in the nest.
   5. One (**cup**) is on the desk.

Activity 5. Read the sentences and fill in both blanks.

   1. Dad had one (**pen**), and Mom had two (**pens**).
   2. Greg takes one (**pill**), and Tom takes three (**pills**).
   3. Bill has two (**dogs**), but I have one (**dog**).
   4. Jim has one red (**van**), but Tim has three (**vans**).

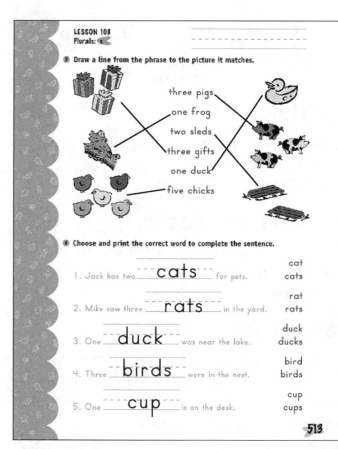

Activity 6. Choose the correct phrase to match the picture. Print the words under the picture.

Pictures: **two dogs, four frogs**
one hat, two crabs

Activity 7. Read the sentences together. Have the student draw a line from the picture to the sentence it matches.

Pictures:

My mother and father go to church on Sunday.
Barb put the butter on the table for dinner.
Herb can hear the buzzer at the door.
The boxer was in the ring to start the match.
Kerr is a good singer.
The red car is a better car than the green one.
Fern put the paper on the chart.
We had the joker in the deck of cards.

Lesson 109 - Plurals: -es

Overview:

- Introduce use of **-es** as plural ending
- Spelling

Materials and Supplies:

- Teacher's Guide & Student Workbook
- White board
- Reader 3: *Counting Trip*

Teaching Tips:

Introduce the use of **-es** when making a plural root word that ends in **ss**, **sh**, **ch** or **x**. Use the white board to illustrate.

Activity 1. Introduce the plural rule: Add **-es** to root words ending in **ss**, **sh**, **ch** or **x**. Discuss the pictures with the student and the reason in each word for the plural addition. Have the student circle the pictures that show it is plural.

Pictures: **two dishes, two benches
two inches, four brushes
three glasses, two peaches,
two axes
two passes**

Activity 2. Spell the words beside each picture. If there is more than one object in the picture, print an **-es** at the end of the word.

Pictures:	I box	**2 boxes**
	1 fox	**4 foxes**
	1 glass	**3 glasses**
	1 ax	**2 axes**
	1 fish	**3 fishes**

Activity 3. Draw a line from the phrase to the picture it matches.

Pictures: **two boxes, two axes, three watches, one kiss, two inches, five bunches**

Activity 4. Read the sentences and words together. Have the student choose and print the correct word to complete the sentence.

1. Mom wanted to mail two (**boxes**) to Jan.
2. There were three (**bunches**) of grapes.
3. Bill had one (**kiss**) from his mom.
4. Jane has three pretty (**dresses**).
5. There were two (**lunches**) on the desk.

Activity 5. Fill in both blanks.

Bill rode one (**bus**), but Jean rode three (**buses**).
Peg broke four (**dishes**). Nan broke two more (**dishes**).
One (**fox**) ran fast, but four (**foxes**) were not fast.

Activity 6. Choose the correct phrase to match the picture. Print the words under the picture.

Pictures: **two dresses, two foxes, four inches, three glasses**

Activity 7. Follow the letters to connect the dots to make a picture.

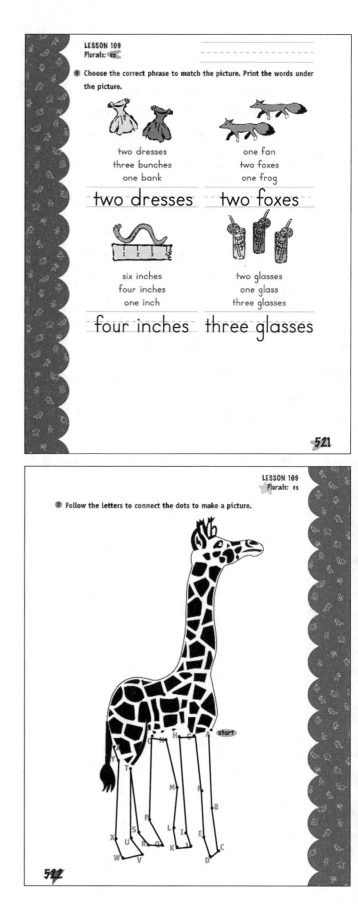

Lesson 110 - Plural: Change y to i + es

Overview:
- Introduce plural root words – **y** ending

Materials and Supplies:
- Teachers Manual & Student Workbook
- White board
- Reader 3: *Jim's Pets*

Teaching Tips:

Introduce the rule: When a word ends in **y**, its plural is formed by changing the **y** to **i**, and adding **es**. Example: **cry – cries**; **baby – babies**; **party – parties**. Use the white board to illustrate.

Activity 1. Study the pictures and discuss which are plural. Have the student put a circle around the pictures that show it is plural (or more than one).

Pictures: **l baby, 2 candies, 2 jars 4 puppies, 2 cherries, 1 daisy**

Activity 2. Spell the word beside the picture where there are two or more objects in the picture. Change the **y** to **i** and add **es**.

1 dolly   3 **dollies**

Activity 3. On the white board, have the student spell the word in singular form. Then cross out the **y** and substitute an **i** in its place, and add **es**. When he is comfortable with the process, have do it independently in his workbook. The student will spell the words under each picture where there are two or more objects in the picture. Change the **y** to **i** and add **es**.

Pictures:	l baby	**2 babies**
	1 cherry	**3 cherries**
	1 cry	**3 cries**
	1 party	**2 parties**
	1 kitty	**3 kitties**

Activity 4. Draw a line from the phrase to the picture it matches.

Pictures: **four puppies running**
two happy dollies
two babies crying
read the funnies
three ladies sitting

Activity 5. Read the sentences together. Have the student choose and print the correct word to complete the sentence.

1. We had three (**candies**) on the plate.
2. Dick went to two (**parties**).
3. The little tot (**cries**) so much.
4. Three (**puppies**) ran to the gate.
5. Both (**babies**) are in the crib.

Activity 6. Choose the correct phrase to match the picture. Print the words under the picture.

Pictures: **two babies, three ladies**
two kitties, one puppy

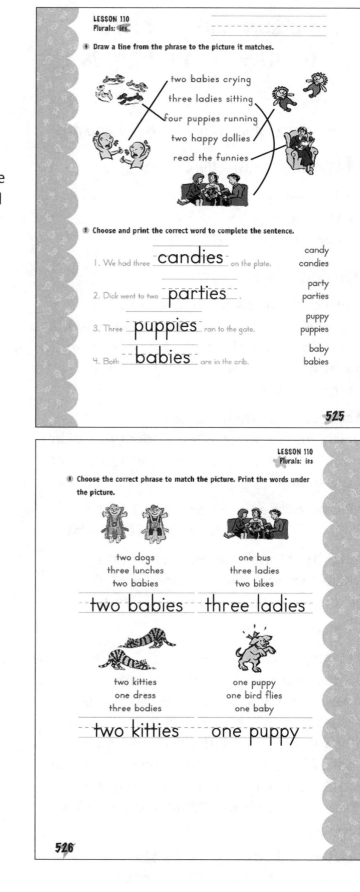

Lesson 111 - Review
Plurals: s, es

Overview:

- Review plurals – **s, es**
- Spelling
- Following written directions

Materials and Supplies:

- Teacher's Guide & Student Workbook
- White board
- Reader 3: *The Baby Parade*

Teaching Tips:

Instruct the student to be aware of the directions for each activity – underline, circle, or put an **x**. On all of the pictures, be sure he has the correct picture in mind.

Activity 1. Put a circle around the pictures that show it is plural.

Pictures: **1 purse, 2 horses, 1 baby, 2 dogs**
3 cats, 1 clock, 1 ball, 2 bibs

Activity 2. Underline the pictures that show it is plural.

Pictures: **2 benches, 2 fishes, 2 churches 1 peach, 2 lunches, 1 desk, 2 foxes, 2 glasses**

Activity 3. Put an **x** on the pictures if they do **NOT** show plurals.

Pictures: **1 lamp, 3 pens, 2 babies, 2 parties 3 ladies, 1 bag, 3 kitties, 8 cookies**

Activity 4. Draw a line from the plural to the word that means just one (singular).

Words: **boxes, box**
cows, cow
bags, bag
babies, baby
punches, punch

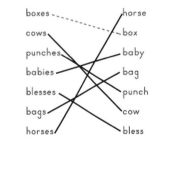

blesses, bless
horses, horse

Activity 5. Study the words together and have the student identify rule for the plural spelling before he prints it in the workbook. Then have the student print the plural form of the following words.

Words:

cat/**cats**	hand/**hands**
pig/**pigs**	bib/**bibs**
fish/**fishes**	wish/**wishes**
fox/**foxes**	box/**boxes**
bench/**benches**	perch/**perches**
dress/**dresses**	press/**presses**
cry/**cries**	baby/**babies**

Activity 6. Read the sentences together. Have the student draw a line from the picture to match the sentence. Underline all the words that are plural.

Pictures: **The benches are painted green.**
The babies will eat the mush.
The boys play in the yard.
The boxes are full of toys.
The birds are singing.
Mom has pretty skirts.

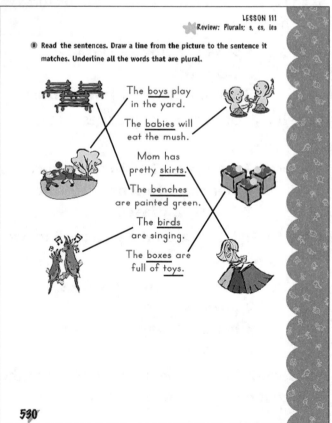

Horizons Kindergarten Phonics

Lesson 112 - Double Vowels: ee

Overview:

- Review double vowel rule
- Rhyming words
- Spelling
- Alphabetical order

Materials and Supplies:

- Teacher's Guide & Student Workbook
- White board
- Reader 3: *The Buzzing Bee*

Teaching Tips:

Review the Double Vowel Rule: When two vowels are close together, the first one is long (says its own name) and the second one is silent. Use the white board to show examples.

Activity 1. Study the pictures together. Have the student put a circle around those you hear the long **e** sound.

Pictures: **meet, bee, chain, beet green, see, sheep, maid float, wheel, feet, teeth**

Activity 2. On the lines below, print the words that match the picture. Cross out the second vowel and make a straight line over the first vowel to show that it has a long sound.

Pictures: **cheék, creék, greét greén, deép, meét queén, feéd, treé**

Activity 3. Draw a line from the word to match the picture.

Pictures: **sweep, sheet, breeze, peek, sheep**

Activity 4. Print the words in alphabetical order.

Words: **cheek, peek, tree, weed**

Activity 5. Read the make-up words.

Make-up Words: **sleed, breem, creef, wheen**

Activity 6. Draw a line from the puzzle phrase to the picture it matches.

Pictures: **sheep in a deep creek
sweep the green street
a seed on the queen's heel
three eels in a tree**

Activity 7. Read the sentences together. Have the student draw a line under the one that matches the picture.

Dad will use a rod when he fishes.
Brad will use a red book when he reads.

Dave will sleep in the street.
Bob ran down the street to meet Lee.

Jill will make green grass for dinner.
Mom can fix beef for lunch.

The candy is too sweet to eat.
Three girls can play the game.

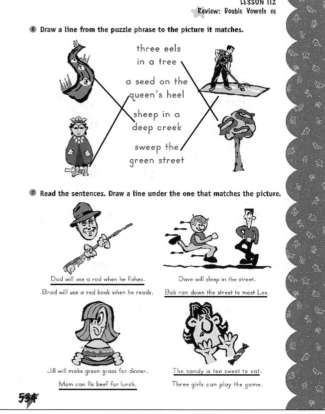

Activity 8. Study the pictures and discuss the spelling for each. Have the student spell the words under the pictures by filling in the beginning and ending sounds.

Pictures: **wee**d, **sh**ee**t**, **ch**ee**k**
pee**k**, **tr**ee, **sw**ee**p**
blee**d**, **wh**ee**l**

Activity 9. Print the words that rhyme.

Words: wheel/**peel, feel, reel**
seed/**need, feed, deed**
sleep/**creep, beep, peep**
cheek/**creek, peek, sleek**
bee/**see, free, tree**

Activity 10. Draw a picture of something from the word bank above.

Lesson 113 - Review Double Vowels: ee, oa & Apostrophe

Overview:

- Review double vowels – **ee**, **oa**
- Rhyming words
- Spelling
- Apostrophe showing possession

Materials and Supplies:

- Teacher's Guide & Student Workbook
- White board
- Reader 3: *Dee Can Walk*

Teaching Tips:

Use the white board to review marking long vowels. Introduce **s** to show possession of one person. Show possession of two or more by using **s**.

Activity 1. Review double vowel **ee** and **oa**. Study the pictures together. Have the student CIRCLE the pictures that have the sound of long **o**. Put a SQUARE around the pictures that have the sound of long **e**.

Long **o**: **boat, float, groan, soap**
Long **e**: **beet, feet, green, sleep**

Activity 2. Study the vocabulary words for meaning. Have the student print the words from the word bank in columns.

Long **o**: **coat, coal, goat, coach, groan, foal**

Long **e**: **weep, feed, creep, seed, feet, three**

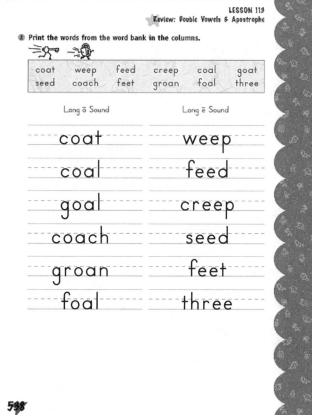

Activity 3. Read the sentences together. Have the student choose and print the correct word on the lines in the sentences.

1. The baby can (**creep**) to the steps.
2. We saw a (**goat**) eat the corn.
3. The man made a (**speech**) after lunch.
4. The (**coach**) helped the team play.

Activity 4. Print the words that rhyme.

Words: coat/**goat, float, boat**
      deep/**peep, creep, seep**

Activity 5. Spell the words by filling in the double vowel **oa** or **ee** under the pictures below.

Pictures: g**oa**t, f**ee**d, t**oa**d
      s**oa**p, r**oa**st, b**ee**t
      ch**ee**k, str**ee**t, r**oa**d

LESSON 113
Review: Double Vowels & Apostrophe

③ Print the correct word on the lines in the sentences.

1. The baby can ___creep___ to the steps.   creep / sleep
2. We saw a ___goat___ eat the corn.   goat / groan
3. The man made a ___speech___ after lunch.   speech / teeth
4. The ___coach___ helped the team play.   coach / catch

④ Print the words that rhyme.

| goat | peep | creep | float | seep | boat |

coat   goat   float   boat
deep   peep   creep   seep

539

LESSON 113
Review: Double Vowels & Apostrophe

⑤ Spell the words by filling in the double vowel oa or ee under the pictures below.

g oa t   f ee d   t oa d

s oa p   r oa st   b ee t

ch ee k   stree t   r oa d

540

Activity 6. Introduce the use of an apostrophe to show possession. Use the white board to illustrate the use of **s** for the possession of one person or thing. Explain the necessity of having to change the structure of a sentence. Have the student change and print the following sentences to show possession of one person or thing. Be sure to use an apostrophe.

1. The bird has blue wings.
   The (**bird's**) wings are blue.

2. Jack has a big coat.
   (**Jack's**) coat is big.

3. The old man has a bent leg.
   The old (**man's**) leg is bent.

Activity 7. Use the same process to illustrate showing possession of two or more persons or things. Have the student identify how many items are involved in each sentence, noting that the word **all** means more than one.

1. The three dogs have old houses.
   The three (**dogs'**) houses are old.

2. All of the goats have sharp horns.
   All of the (**goats'**) horns are sharp.

3. The birds have nests in the trees.
   The (**birds'**) nests are in the trees.

LESSON 113
Review: Double Vowels & Apostrophe

This mark ' is an apostrophe.
It is used before the s at the end of a word to show that something belongs to one person or thing. This is called possession. It is used as s' to show that something belongs to two or more persons or things.
Examples: (One person or thing)
This shirt belongs to Bob. ⟶ This is Bob's shirt
The cat has yellow fur. ⟶ The cat's fur is yellow.
Jack has a red car. ⟶ Jack's car is red.

① Change and print the following sentences to show possession of one person or thing. Be sure to use an apostrophe.

1. The bird has blue wings.

The ___bird's___ wings are blue.

2. Jack has a big coat.

___Jack's___ coat is big.

3. The old man has a bent leg.

The old ___man's___ leg is bent.

541

LESSON 113
Review: Double Vowels & Apostrophe

⑦ Change and print the following sentences to show possession of two or more persons or things. Be sure to use an apostrophe.

1. The three dogs have old houses.

The three ___dogs'___ houses are old.

2. All of the goats have sharp horns.

All of the ___goats'___ horns are sharp.

3. The birds have nests in the trees.

The ___birds'___ nests are in the trees.

542

Horizons Kindergarten Phonics

Lesson 114 - Review Double Vowels: ai, ea

Overview:

- Review double vowels – **ai, ea**
- Review apostrophe for singular and plural possession
- Sentence completion

Materials and Supplies:

- Teacher's Guide & Student Workbook
- White board
- Reader 3: *The Snow Trail*

Teaching Tips:

Review double vowels: **ai, ea**. Review apostrophe as used for singular and plural possession.

Activity 1. Study the pictures and discuss the vocabulary meaning of each. Have the student put a CIRCLE around the pictures that have the sound of long **a**. Put a SQUARE around the pictures that have the sound of long **e**.

Long **a: grain, stain, snail**
Long **e: meat, beat, speak, queen, team**

Activity 2. Print the words from the word bank in the long **a** and long **e** columns.

Words:	Long **a** sound	Long **e** sound
	quail	**Dean**
	rail	**real**
	train	**bean**
	trail	**deal**
	rain	**meal**
	mail	**seam**

Activity 3. Read the sentences together. Have the student choose and print the correct word on the line in the sentence.

1. It is fun to ride on a (**train**).
2. Jean saw a mother (**quail**).

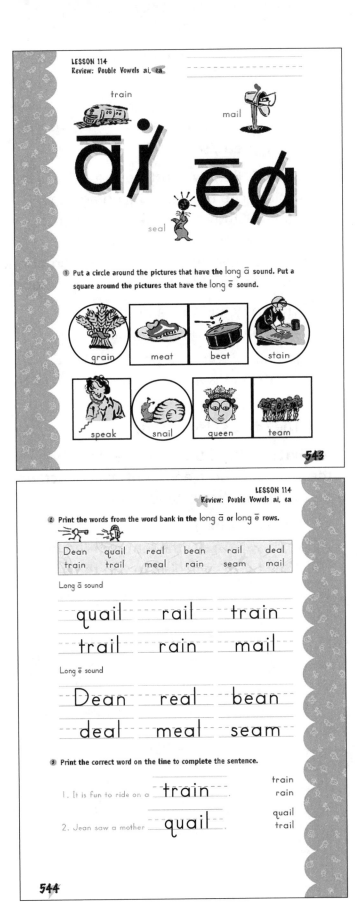

Activity 4. Spell the words by filling in the double vowels **ai** or **ea**.

> Pictures: st**ea**m, tr**ai**n, r**ai**n
> m**ai**l, s**ea**l, s**ai**l
> tr**ea**t, s**ea**t, b**ai**t

Activity 5. Review apostrophe for singular possession. Use the white board again for illustration. Study the sentences together. Have the student change and print the following sentences to show possession of one person or thing. Be sure to use an apostrophe.

1. The baby has a little bottle.
   The (**baby's**) bottle is little.

2. Jim has a dog for a pet.
   (**Jim's**) pet is a dog.

3. The dog has a leg that hurts.
   The (**dog's**) leg is hurt.

Activity 6. Read the sentences together. Have the student choose and print the correct word on the line in the sentence.

1. You can (**deal**) the cards.
2. Faith will (**mail**) the letters in the box.
3. The (**team**) will plan to win the game.

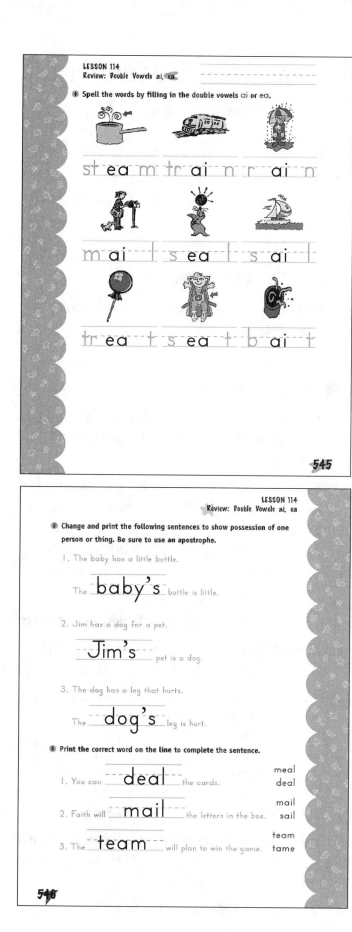

Horizons Kindergarten Phonics

Lesson 115 - Review All Double Vowels

Overview:

• Review all double vowels

Materials and Supplies:

• Teacher's Guide & Student Workbook
• White board
• Reader 3: *The Puppet Show*

Teaching Tips:

Study and discuss all the pictures so that the student is able to identify them.

Activity 1. Look at the pictures below. Put a circle around those where you hear the long **a** sound.

Pictures: **maid, paid, team, braid
mail, grain, jail, train**

Activity 2. Look at the pictures below. Put a circle around those where you hear the long **e** sound.

Pictures: **beet, heat, meat, goat
peel, pail, leap, sleep**

Activity 3. Look at the pictures below. Put a circle around those where you hear the long **o** sound.

Pictures: **toad, soap, bride, road
lake, float, goat, boat**

Activity 4. Read the make-up words.

Make-up Words: **claip, steeb, greap, sloaj**

Activity 5. Draw a line from the puzzle phrase to the picture it matches.

Pictures: **jeans on a goat
a boat on a wheel
a train on a tree
the meat on a chair**

Activity 6. On the lines below, print the words that match the pictures. Cross out the second vowel, and make a straight line over the first vowel to show that it has a long sound.

Pictures: **cōa̶l, trē e̶, chē e̶k**
spē a̶k, rōa̶d, mā i̶d
crē e̶k, chā i̶n, rā i̶n

Activity 7. Read the sentences together. Have the student choose and print the correct word on the lines in the sentence.

1. Jane has (**cheeks**) that are pink.
2. The (**sheep**) have grass to eat.
3. I see a ship that (**floats**) on the lake.
4. The (**train**) was on the rail.
5. Don has a (**seat**) on the bus.
6. It is too deep to swim in the (**creek**).
7. Gail went out in the (**rain**) and got wet.
8. The (**boat**) will float when we ride on it.

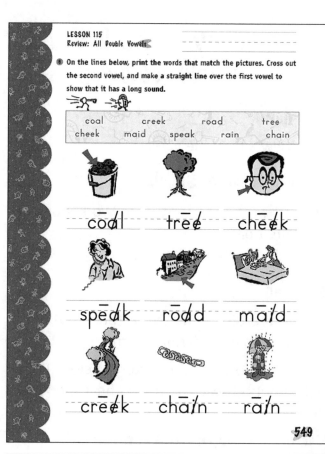

Activity 8. Spell the words by filling in the double vowels **ee**, **oa**, **ea**, or **ai**.

> Pictures: tr**ee**, r**ea**d, b**ea**n
> t**ai**l, b**oa**t, f**ee**t
> s**ea**t, s**ee**, d**ee**p
> c**oa**ch, s**ai**l, t**oa**st

Activity 9. Review the apostrophe for plural possession. Again use the white board to illustrate plural possession. Have the student change and print the following sentence to show possession of two or more persons or things. Be sure to use an apostrophe.

1. The four cats sleep in big beds.
   Four (**cats'**) beds are big.

2. All of the sheep have soft wool.
   All of the (**sheeps'**) wool is soft.

3. The hens have nests in the pen.
   The (**hens'**) nests are in the pen.

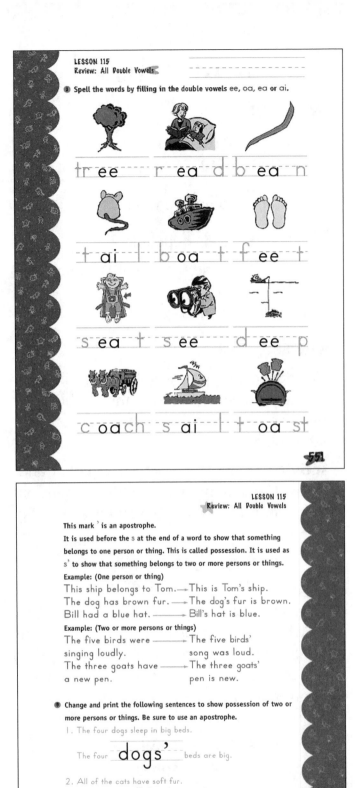

Lesson 116 - Digraph ay

Overview:

- Introduce digraph **ay**
- Rhyming words
- Spelling
- Sentence comprehension

Materials and Supplies:

- Teacher's Guide & Student Workbook
- White board
- Reader 3: *Ice Hockey*

Teaching Tips:

Introduce digraph **ay**, noting that the **y** is used as a vowel and follows the double vowel rule: The first vowel is long and the second one is silent.

Activity 1. Study the pictures together and discuss the digraph **ay**. Have the student put a circle around those where you hear the long **a** sound.

Pictures: **tray, jay, bug, play**
pray, trap, spray, Kay

Activity 2. Study the pictures together. Use the white board to demonstrate crossing out the second vowel **y** and making a straight line over the first vowel to show it has the long sound of **a**. Then have the student do his work in the workbook alone.

Pictures: **Fāy̶, trāy̶, prāy̶**
pāy̶, Kāy̶, sprāy̶
clāy̶, stāy̶, grāy̶

Activity 3. Read the make-up words.

Make-up Words: **snay, tay, glay, chay**

Activity 4. Print the words that rhyme.

play/**say, bay, lay**
meet/**beet, feet, greet**
best/**rest, nest, test**
past/**mast, cast, last**
feed/**deed, need, heed**
cake/**take, lake, bake**
bug/**tug, lug, rug**

Activity 5. Read the puzzle phrases together and discuss the meaning. Have the student draw a line from the puzzle phrase to the picture it matches.

Pictures: **lost the way to the bay**
         spray the hay
         a jay in the clay
         a weed on a tray

Activity 6. Spell the words under the pictures by filling the **ay** sound.

Pictures: J**ay**, tr**ay**, cl**ay**, pl**ay**

Activity 7. Put the words in alphabetical order.

Words: **clay, day, May, stay**

Activities 8 & 9. Read the sentences together. Have the student draw a line under the one that matches the picture. Then print the correct sentence on the lines below.

Jay can play the game.

Jay can play the tray.

The sheep will pray and then eat.

The sheep will eat the hay.

Fay had a good day in her boat at the bay.

Fay had a clay day with her boat at the bay.

We saw a lady with green hair.

We saw a lady with gray hair.

Horizons Kindergarten Phonics

Lesson 117 - Digraph ey

Overview:

- Introduce digraph **ey**
- Alphabetical order
- Sentence comprehension

Materials and Supplies:

- Teacher's Guide & Student Workbook
- White board
- Reader 3: *Field Hockey*

Teaching Tips:

Introduce digraph **ey**, noting that the **y** is used as a vowel and follows the double vowel rule: The first vowel is long and the second one is silent.

Activity 1. Study the pictures together and discuss the digraph **ey**. Have the student put a circle around those that have the long **e** sound.

Pictures: **monkey, donkey, vest, money valley, hockey, man, key**

Activity 2. On the lines below, print the words that match the pictures. Cross out the second vowel (of the digraph) and make a straight line over the first vowel to show that it has the long **e** sound.

Pictures/Words: **kēy, monkēy, monēy hockēy, vallēy, donkēy**

Activity 3. Look at the pictures together. Have the student listen for the long **e** sound in the words. Draw a line from the pictures that rhyme.

donkey/**monkey**
see/**tree**
deep/**sheep, sleep**
seen/**clean, bean, green**

Activity 4. Read the sentences together. Have the student draw a line from the picture to the sentence that tells about the word.

1. This is another name for dimes, nickels, quarters, and dollars. (**money**)
2. This is a game that is played on the ice. (**hockey**)
3. This is an animal that lives in the zoo. (**monkey**)
4. This is a place between two or more mountains. (**valley**)
5. This is something that will open or lock doors. (**key**)
6. This is an animal that usually lives on a farm. (**donkey**)

Activity 5. Print the words from Exercise 4.

hockey, money, valley, monkey, key, donkey

Activity 6. Read the make-up words.

Make-up Words: **rey, bley, stey, chey**

Activity 7. Draw a line from the puzzle phrase to the picture it matches.

Pictures: **a monkey with money**
a key for a fish
a donkey in a tree
a hockey player with a football

Activity 8. Print the words in alphabetical order.

Words: **donkey, key, money, valley**

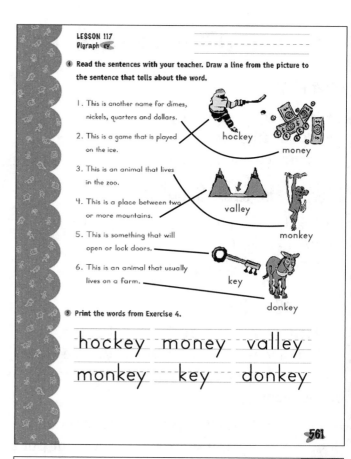

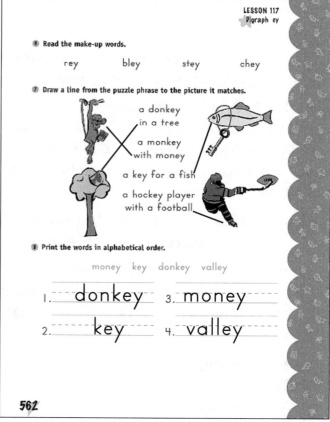

Lesson 118 - Review
Digraphs ay, ey

Overview:
- Review digraphs **ay**, **ey**
- Review apostrophe – possession

Materials and Supplies:
- Teacher's Guide & Student Workbook
- White board
- Reader 3: *Monkeys*

Teaching Tips:
Review digraphs **ey**, **ay**. Have the student note that the rule for **ay** and **ey** is the same as the double vowel rule: the second vowel is silent, and the first one is long and says its own name.

Activity 1. Put a CIRCLE around the words that have the sound of long **a**. Put a SQUARE around the words that have the long sound of **e**.

Long **a**: **play, clay, x-ray, day**
Long **e**: **key, money, monkey, donkey**

Activity 2. Read the sentences together. Have the student choose and print the correct word to complete the sentence.

1. I get up in the morning each (**day**).
2. The dish was made of red (**clay**).
3. The brown (**monkey**) lives in the zoo.
4. We are wet from the (**spray**) of the hose.
5. Dad has the (**money**) to buy a car.
6. May has a pretty (**gray**) dress.
7. The men can play the (**hockey**) game.
8. We went to church to (**pray**).

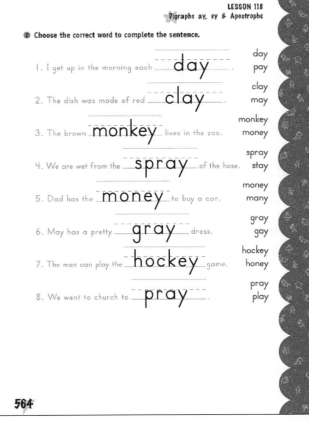

Activity 3. Draw a line from the picture to the word it matches.

    Pictures: **donkey, x-ray**
              play, hockey
              pray, monkey
              spray, tray

Activity 4. Finish spelling the words under the pictures below by finishing with the letters **ay** or **ey**.

    Pictures: donk**ey**, monk**ey**, pr**ay**
              x-r**ay**, k**ey**, hay,
              spr**ay**, hock**ey**, tr**ay**
              pl**ay**, mon**ey**, hon**ey**

124

Activity 5. Review the rule for the apostrophe being used to show possession. Read the sentences with the student and discuss the possession of the person or thing. Have the student change and print the following sentences to show possession of one person or thing. Be sure to use an apostrophe.

1. The tail of the monkey is long.
   The (**monkey's**) tail is long.

2. The rays of the sun are hot.
   The (**sun's**) rays are hot.

3. The handles of the tray are black.
   The (**tray's**) handles are black.

Activity 6. Review the rule for plural possession. Read the sentences with the student and discuss the changes necessary. Have the student change and print the following sentences showing plural possession. Be sure to use an apostrophe.

1. Both tots have new toys.
   The new toys are the (**tots'**). *or*
   The (**tots'**) toys are new.

2. The moles have homes in the dirt.
   The (**moles'**) homes are in the dirt.

3. The gas tanks of all the cars are full.
   All the (**cars'**) gas tanks are full.

4. Both boys have gray monkeys.
   The (**boys'**) monkeys are gray.

Review: An apostrophe is used before the 's in a word to show that something belongs to one person or thing. It is used after the s' to show that something belongs to two or more persons or things.

⑤ Change and print the following sentences to show possession of one person or thing. Be sure to use an apostrophe.

1. The tail of the monkey is long.

The monkey's tail is long.

2. The rays of the sun are hot.

The sun's rays are hot.

3. The handles of the tray are black.

The tray's handles are black.

567

⑥ Change and print the following sentences to show possession of two or more persons or things. Be sure to use an apostrophe.

1. Both tots have new toys.

The tots' toys are new.

2. The moles have homes in the dirt.

The moles' homes are in the dirt.

3. The gas tanks of all the cars are full.

All the cars' gas tanks are full.

4. Both boys have gray monkeys.

The boys' monkeys are gray.

568

Horizons Kindergarten Phonics

125

Lesson 119 - Diphthong ow

Overview:

- Introduce diphthong **ow**
- Sentence comprehension

Materials and Supplies:

- Teacher's Guide & Student Workbook
- White board
- Reader 3: *Grandpa's Surprise for Floyd and Dow*

Teaching Tips:

Introduce the diphthong **ow**, making note that it has two sounds: (1) as in **cow**, and (2) as in **slow**.

Activity 1. Introduce the Diphthong Rule: **ow** is a set of two vowel sounds blended as in the word **cow**. It also makes the sound you hear in the word **slow** as a long **o**.

Study the pictures together and discuss the sound of **ow** in each. Have the student put a circle around the picture if it has the **ow** sound as in **cow**.

> Pictures: **crown, owl, frown, goat clown, howl, pen, cow**

Activity 2. Study the pictures and words together. Discuss the meaning of each for vocabulary development. Have the student draw a line from the picture to the word it matches.

> Pictures: **town, crown, clown, cow, brown, plow**

Activity 3. Study the pictures and words together. Discuss the meaning of each for vocabulary development. Have a student put a SQUARE around the picture if it has the **ow** sound as in **slow** with a long **o**.

> Pictures: **blow, stamp, crow, elbow, snow, bowl, flip, throw**

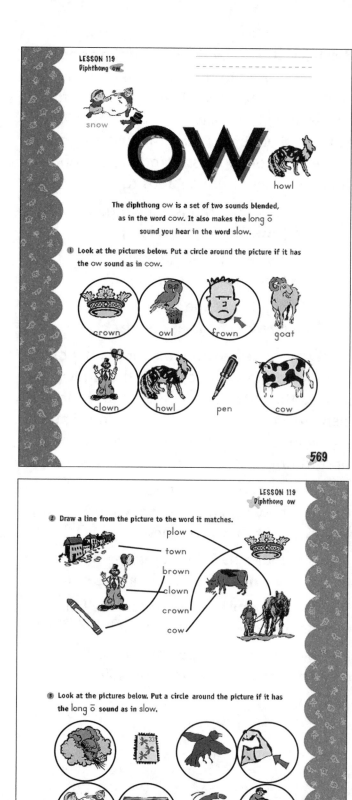

Activity 4. Study the words and pictures together. Have the student draw a line from the picture to the word it matches.

Pictures: **show, elbow, crow, throw, snow, bowl**

Activity 5. Read the sentences together. Have the student print the correct word on the line in the sentence.

1. Dad will (**mow**) the grass in the back yard.
2. Owen fell down and hurt his (**elbow**).
3. We saw pretty colors in the (**rainbow**).
4. Don can (**throw**) the ball in the game.
5. We will go to the (**show**) to see the clown.
6. The boys and girls will play in the (**snow**) with the sleds.

Activity 6. Read one word from each of the boxes and have the student put a circle around the correct word in each box.

Words: **crow, mow, brown**
frown, show, throw
clown, how, slow
grow, crown, elbow

Activity 7. Read the sentences together. Have the student print the correct word on the line in the sentence.

1. Mom drove to (**town**) in a red truck.
2. Jake has some short (**brown**) pants.
3. The wings on the (**owl**) were broken.
4. The queen's (**crown**) had many stones in it.
5. Mike, the (**clown**), made us smile.
6. I want to see (**how**) Mom makes the cake.

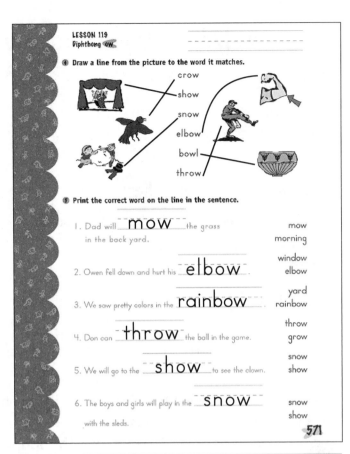

Lesson 120 - Diphthong ou

Overview:

- Introduce diphthong **ou**
- Sentence comprehension
- Nouns

Materials and Supplies:

- Teacher's Guide & Student Workbook
- White board
- Reader 3: *The House Mouse*

Teaching Tips:

Introduce the diphthong **ou**, making note that it has to sounds: (1) as in **out**, and (2) as in **you**.

Activity 1. Introduce the Diphthong Rule: **ou** is a set of two vowel sounds blended as you hear in the word **out**. It also makes the sound you in the word **you**. Study the pictures together and discuss the sound of **ou** in each. Have the student put a CIRCLE around the picture if it has the **ou** sound as in **out**.

   Pictures: **mouse, ouch, swim, scout count, cloud, loud, north**

Activity 2. Print the **ou** sound in the words under the pictures.

   Pictures: cl**ou**d, m**ou**nt, r**ou**nd
         ouch, fl**ou**r, c**ou**ch
         m**ou**th, **ou**tside, s**ou**nd

                        Horizons Kindergarten Phonics

Activity 3. Study the sentences together. Have the student print the correct word on the line in the sentences.

1. Jane has a (**pound**) of grapes.
2. She will take (**our**) dog for a fast run.
3. The cat will (**crouch**) when he wants to catch a mouse.
4. We made a (**round**) mark on the chart.
5. The rat made a hole in the (**ground**).
6. The apple was too (**sour**) for our mouth.
7. The (**scout**) will help set up the tents.

Activity 4. The diphthong **ou** blended together can also make the sound we hear in the word **you**. Print the **ou** sound in the words under the pictures.

Pictures: c**ou**gar, s**ou**p, gr**ou**p, w**ou**nd

Activity 5. Study the pictures and words together. Discuss the meaning for each to increase vocabulary development. Have the student put a SQUARE around the pictures that have the sound you hear in the word **you**.

Pictures: **wound, camp, mail, soup
goat, yes, group, cougar**

Activity 6. Study the sentences together. Have the student print the correct word on the line in the sentences.

    1. (**You**) are to fill in the words on the lines.
    2. Mom can fix some (**soup**) for our lunch.
    3. The (**cougar**) can bite you.

Activity 7. Read the sentences with the students, reminding them to include appropriate capitalization and punctuation. Have the students print the sentences on the lines provided.

    Sentences: **I** like to do a lot of reading.
                 What do you like to do for fun**?**

Activity 8. Review nouns with the students. Read the nouns that name a thing, then draw a line from the picture to the word it matches.

    Pictures: **mouth, wound, cougar, couch, soup**

Activity 9. Review nouns with the students. Read the nouns that name a thing, then draw a line from the picture to the word it matches.

    Pictures: **snow, crown, elbow, clown, cow**

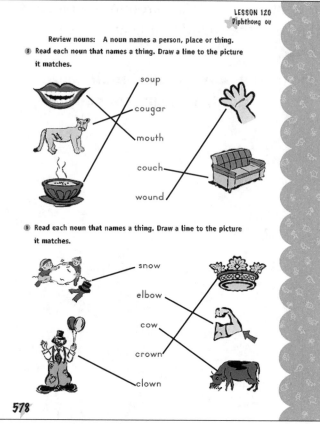